# LIFE UNDER PRESSURE

## Moving Beyond Financial Meltdown

## Sherman S. Smith, Ph.D.

Heritage
Builders
Helping You Build a Family of Faith

# ACKNOWLEDGEMENT

I wish to thank the members of the Sonrise Baptist Church for their unwavering support of my ministry.

I wish to thank the partners of Heritage Builders, Otis Ledbetter, Jim Weidmann, and Kurt Bruner for allowing me to become a part of such a great organization.

I wish to thank Justin Davis for his untiring work in helping facilitate all the duties necessary to bring a project together.

I wish to thank Keith Bennett and the staff of Valley Type & Design for the great art work and formatting to make this book a success.

I wish to thank my new editor Amy Van Vleck for the painstaking work and untiring devotion she dedicated to this important work.

Published in Clovis, California by Heritage Builders, LLC and distributed in the United States and Worldwide by BookSurge, Inc.

Scripture quotations are from The Holy Bible, **KING JAMES VERSION.**

Library of Congress Cataloging-in-Publication Data

Smith, Sherman

Life Under Pressure, Moving Beyond Financial Meltdown/ Sherman Smith

Includes bibliographic references

ISBN 0-61-530423-0

Printed in the United States of America

# DEDICATION

To Kathy Ann Smith.

# TABLE OF CONTENTS

# PREFACE

I am trying to make this book timeless because of its Biblical message. However, at this time, we are in a deep recession that is going to worsen over the next few years or longer. The practical applications in this book will be worth preserving in the heart and mind for generations. You will notice during the course of this book that I relied on resources from the mid-1990s. I wanted to go back 10 to 15 years to get the perspective of what was predicted for the future and what is happening at the present. It is a great barometer to measure what is ahead.

We have been through economic downturns and at least two major depressions (1878,1929-1932). Every seven to 10 years since 1910, we experience recession as the economy corrects itself. In our country, this is nothing new. However, Americans get comfortable in their prosperity and forget the hard times, if they have been through them at all.

Now, a new generation of folks are going through a deep recession for the first time of memory, and the struggle is affecting every facet of their lives, whether it is marriage, family management, or business. As a result, it is driving good and bad decision making.

The Chicken Littles are at it again. The Internet is full of nonsense about the demise and break-up of America. This is my fourth writing dealing with this paranoia. The first was my Doctoral Dissertation about how Doomsayer Literature creates paranoia in the general population. From that came the bestseller, *Exploding the Doomsday Money Myths, Why It's Not Time To Panic*, which dealt with the paranoia created by books written in the mid-1990s, both secular and Christian, predicting the demise of America some time in that decade, which of course never happened.

I wrote *Lie 2K: Why the Alleged End-of-the-World Year-2000 Computer Crisis is Really Just a Hoax*, and who won't remember the paranoia created by pundits of gloom? America and the world were supposed to fall into the Second Coming of Jesus Christ as they pegged the computer crises to the end of the world. People were storing food and hiding out, preparing to survive after the devastation of computer crashes hit the planet. As a guest on Ollie North's nationally syndicated radio program on New Year's Eve 1999, we waited for the final countdown and had this conversation:

"What are you doing this evening, Dr. Smith?" Ollie asked tongue-in-cheek.

"I have turned over my car in the yard and set it on fire so that we won't get hit by the neighbors looking for food," I replied.

"I love this guy!" Ollie exclaimed to millions of listeners.

My partner, Buddy Kingston, was in Bethlehem on New Year's Eve. He sent a message to me: "Jesus didn't come, and the lights are still on in Bethlehem!"

Well Jesus did not return, and that era is a bygone history that has left its proponents of doom embarrassed once again. Although I take what is happening seriously, my reaction to the opinion that we are surely "heading down the tubes" this time is with the same emotion as when I wrote those books refuting the paranoia created by these hard times.

I have not been wrong yet, and I won't be wrong this time. When God gets through evangelizing the planet, He will destroy this nation. (That time has not yet come unless He comes, which He might, but we don't know that.) All the prognosticators and forecasters of the Biblical world have been wrong in the past, and they will miss the mark again and again. Why? Because God is not leaking His private information to an elite few.

So why am I so confident? Is it my superior education? Superior experience? Superior intelligence? It is none of these things because I am not superior in any of them. Unlike so many who will disagree — or those economists and financial engineers who won't buy into a thing I say — I am pegging my entire philosophy on two things.

First, the future is unknown, but we can understand and have peace about some of the future by looking at what's happened in the past. This is something many economists and financial gurus, who are scaring you to death, completely fail to do when dealing with their forecasts.

Second, I stand on what I believe to be the Biblical foundation of truth. When America has fallen, it will be because God has finished His work in this country. He has used America to evangelize the world and when that is done, the world of Christians will be gone. What is happening now may have everything to do with end times, but I believe the end of time will be much worse than what we are enduring presently: this is a picnic compared to what will happen.

So what do we do? We better live like Jesus is coming back at any second — because He could. We better plan like He never is, and have our finances in order for the here and now. Therein lies a formula that will help you stay in fellowship with God while keeping your financial feet on solid ground.

We are a country of sinful men and women who make sinful mistakes. We are also a country of Christian men and women who love the Lord. There does not exist the consistency and quality of Christian life anywhere in the world like in America. God will protect His people in this terrible economic climate because He is not finished yet. When He is, you will know it by the sound of a trumpet. The post-tribulation, mid-tribulation and post-millennium preachers can revel in the signs all they want, but Christ will come "as a thief in the night." These guys tend to miss this fundamental truth, which is right under their noses, while they stumble making dates, remaking dates, setting times, resetting times, and drive themselves senseless trying to make it all work.

This book is full of practical advice that will help you no matter what the economic climate. I hope to encourage you, prepare you, and generally help you — because this will happen again.

# CHAPTER ONE

## PRESSED FOR CASH

When I was a kid, people would ask my Dad, "Why is he so short?" (I finally did grow to medium height.)

Dad would reply, "Sherm was born in a Kansas farmhouse, we were poor and had no electricity. His mother had no incubator, so she put him in a pressure cooker!"

That philosophy held true. I have been "in the pressure cooker" most of my life. Someone once said it like this: "Suffering is suffering, and it doesn't matter a whole lot how you suffer." That is true.

When you are suffering, the kind of suffering matters little. I don't believe there is any more brutal suffering than when a person endures financial pressure.

When someone dies, there is great bereavement, but you can get over the loss of a loved one in time. Health problems are nagging, but at least we can in most cases get relief from the stress of the illness. Marriage problems can be persistent, but through counseling and even divorce, a person can recuperate.

When it comes to money, the situation is vastly different. Bad decisions can be not only ongoing but also lifelasting. Millions of families and individuals suffer trauma inflicted by the financial pressure cooker.

If you are in a financial bind, then I don't need to tell you what it's like. The constant nagging, gut-wrenching despair keeps you awake at night, resulting in painful sleeplessness. Arising in the morning brings no relief as you are forced to face the negatives of the day.

I have counseled with literally hundreds of people over the years who cannot function because of financial stress. It doesn't matter how a person gets into that situation; the point is how to cope with it while you are in it, and how to get out of it.

Being in the "pressure cooker" is no fun. Just ask me.

## High Anxiety

A few years ago, I had ear problems and bronchitis. In spite of several visits to the doctor, I still couldn't shake the infection.

Finally, my doctor asked, "Sherm, what do you do for a living?"

"I'm a stockbroker."

"I believe your problems are related to stress," he said.

"Stress? I have no stress. I love my job."

"It doesn't matter how much you love your job, you are still under a great deal of stress," he countered. "Let me ask you something."

"What job do you think would be number one on a stress chart?" he asked.

I thought for a moment and then said, "An air traffic controller."

The doctor replied, "Good guess, but wrong. The most stressful job in America is a neurosurgeon. First, he must deal with knowing a patient has a 50 percent chance of dying on the operating table. It is not easy to watch a patient with whom you have built a relationship die — especially when you are trying to save his life. Second, he will have to face the family if the person dies; and third, he might endure a lawsuit after losing the patient."

"Boy, I'm glad I'm not a neurosurgeon," I said.

"What do you think is the second most stressful job in America?" he asked.

"An air traffic controller?" I immediately inserted.

He quipped, "A stockbroker."

As his point sunk in, I realized that a doctor may lose a life, but a financial advisor is in danger of losing the life savings. It is one thing to be dead, but it is another to have your entire future wiped out by the decision of one man.

No wonder I was under stress.

I thought about the times I had to make decisions to buy and sell securities based on what I thought would or would not happen to the investment, taking into account the national economy or changes in a company's plans, etc.

No wonder brokers jumped off bridges following the 1929 stock market crash. After the more recent 1987 crash, many quit the business because they could not face their clients.

If the broker feels stress, imagine how the person who lost his life savings feels. In some cases, the loss may not be the broker's fault, but rather the result of the client's decision to invest in something against the broker's advice. Many times, I have advised against an investment only to have the client buy the security anyway.

Aside from investment decisions, other situations can cause the loss of a financial fortune. Without listing those situations, suffice it to say that when the money is gone, or the bank account is about to go dry, severe anxiety results.

## Tallying Up Failure

I can handle almost anything that comes along, but I have difficulty handling the despondency of financial woes. God knows if I need to be on my knees, it will come from the stress put on me by my checking account.

These kinds of pressures occur for several reasons.

*Financial pressures can cause depression.*

The most common source of depression falls on men in their late 30s and entire 40s who have assessed their lives and tallied up failure for one reason or another. Usually, it is because they lack certain material goods and have not – according to their own expectations – reached their goals in life. This assessment is usually arrived at by a comparison with someone in their own economic peer group.

When I was a consultant, I analyzed businesses in trouble and then worked out a plan to fix the problem areas. During this time, I had a dual career as the senior pastor of a Baptist church in California. Because of my experience and education in the business world, I provided financial counseling with private individuals, especially people in the church. I learned a lot about life during those sessions.

One evening I received a phone call from a distressed spouse concerning her husband. It seems he was in dire straights and needed to see me immediately. Because of the frantic pitch of her voice, I agreed.

Later that night, they arrived at my private home office.

"Dr. Smith, I am going to kill myself," the husband said with obvious urgency.

Bewildered, I asked, "Don (fictitious name), what in the world could be going on that would make you want to take your life?"

"I am 41 years old, in debt up to my eyeballs, I don't own a foot of anything, and I'm going to have to file for bankruptcy. My life is over."

What could I say to him that would initiate some relief in this situation? I knew that "cheer up" was not going to work.

"Do you still have your job, Don?" I asked.

"Oh, yes, and he is going to get a promotion!" answered his wife.

Somewhat puzzled, I tried to get to the root of the problem.

In a short time, I concluded that this family was wasting all their resources through a lack of spending discipline.

I was expecting great credit card debts, two or three automobiles, and a mortgage that would choke a horse. Instead, I discovered that these two were making more than $60,000 per year, had only $6,000 in unpaid debt, and had no credit cards.

Their rent payment was well within my financial guidelines, and they had one car paid for and owed very little on another. However, they were behind in all their bills and finding it extremely difficult to make it from one pay check to the next.

## What's Good for the Goose...

Two weeks after the counseling session with Don and Anna, I was faced with another case of bad financial management — one on a much grander scale. A company in Berkeley, California, was considering filing for Chapter 11 Reorganization bankruptcy or possibly shutting down their business and lay off dozens of workers. As an outside consultant, I had been advising the management team for some time.

That day, after leaving them with the prognosis to ponder, I found myself sitting in freeway traffic. With some time to think, I looked up through the sunroof of my BMW while contemplating what I had just said to the board members of this struggling company.

Sitting in their conference room a few minutes earlier, I had responded frankly when the CEO and president asked for my final analysis. Also present in this meeting were the chief financial officer, the executive vice president, and two secretaries. With their jobs hanging in the balance, all had eagerly awaited my response.

"Gentlemen, your parking lot looks like a Mercedes Benz dealership," I had bluntly told them. "You live in multi-million dollar homes in the hills of Berkeley overlooking the beautiful San Francisco Bay, and you have a huge yacht docked at the marina."

Without stopping to consider the ramifications of this straight-forward approach, I barreled on.

"The long and short of all this is: you are taking too much money out of your business to support your luxurious lifestyles, and you are going to put all your people out of work because of the negative cash flow."

A tense quiet descended on the room. Second-guessing my blockbuster approach, I imagined myself being thrown through the window as my briefcase followed me in the air to the parking lot below — hitting me on the head.

It seemed like hours before anyone spoke. Finally, one of the executive secretaries loudly slapped her hand on the conference table and with the other hand pointed at the gentlemen in question. "That's what I've been telling you birds for five years!" she scolded.

I had done my part and, a few moments later, gratefully left through the front door and not the window.

Gridlocked in traffic, I thought about Don and his wife, Anna. "What did I just tell those executives back there?" I asked myself aloud. "I told them their lifestyles were ruining their business."

Then it hit me: What's good for the goose is good for the gander!

In other words, whether it is a multi-million dollar operation or a small family budget, dysfunctional financial problems have their roots in the same dry ground.

"I need to get back to Don and Anna and find out about their personal finances," I advised myself again. "Maybe they have the same problems as this company."

## Debt Free in Ten Months

I set up an interview with Don and Anna and sure enough they had plenty of money; they just didn't know how to handle it.

Don and Anna were entertaining friends almost every night. Their Domino Pizza bill was horrendous. On top of this, they were spending every other weekend at a Lake Tahoe resort and gambling a large portion of their money away playing the slot machines.

I was almost relieved by my diagnosis: They were dysfunctional! I had to help them!

"Don, if I told you that in 10 months you will have $10,000 invested with my firm, that you will be able to give to your church each Sunday, that you will be totally out of debt and on your way to buying a new home within three years, would you believe me?"

"How could you possibly do that?" he questioned.

"If I could do it, would you go along with a plan?"

"If you could do that, I would do anything you asked," he said excitedly.

"Is it all right with you, Anna?" I asked.

She replied, "If you can get us out from under this stress, I'll do anything."

"What I am going to propose will take discipline," I said seriously. "I want your check book. I will prepare your checks, and you can sign and mail them. I want your pay checks each week at my door on Friday evening. I will then allot your spending money for the necessities you must buy. I will call your creditors (which I did) and arrange for a portion of the debt to be paid each pay day."

I waited to see if they were still as excited as they had been moments before. As they looked intently at one another, I could see their heads nodding in agreement.

"Okay," they said.

"Now, here's what I expect from you. There will be zero entertaining for 10 months. You will go nowhere except to and from work, the grocery store, church, and other trips necessary for basic living. Some spending money will be allotted occasionally for your own entertainment at a mid-priced restaurant, but that's about it."

The couple had no children, which made this fairly easy. If they had children, I would have adjusted the plan to take the kids into consideration.

"Don, you and Anna need to learn to be financially functional. If you ever learn how, you will be happy people."

At first they looked at me as if I were crazy and then said, "What do you get for all that work?"

Very calmly and seriously I inserted into their minds that I wanted no remuneration from them except permission to print this story someday in order to drive a message across to thousands of people just like them.

What is that message?

Many Americans are dysfunctional in the social areas of life — particularly in the area of finances. This lack of education about how to properly handle our finances in the home, business, church, and school has caused our country to short circuit. We must do something about it while we can.

> *There are two kinds of people - those who earn interest and those who pay it.*

Every problem imaginable has resulted from America's lack of financial discipline. People steal, lie, cheat, sell drugs, and use all kinds of devious methods to con people. Why? So they can get more money to buy more stuff.

Even those who don't resort to blatant lying and cheating often seek financial help from their relatives or neighbors. This can put tremendous stress on the relationship between the lender and the person who doesn't pay it back. Loaning money to dysfunctional people can result in severe financial pressure.

## Overloaded with New Money

Almost every day at least one person calls me for financial advice. They want to know how to escape from the financial dungeon; and most everyone in this situation is looking for a quick fix, like winning the lottery or inheriting money.

Most people think the quick fix will solve all their financial problems. When dysfunctional people, who have never had money before get "overloaded" with new money, their problems often go from bad to worse. Experience has taught me that just because a person suddenly comes into money doesn't mean he or she will automatically become functional and know how to handle it.

Not long ago, I was contacted by a family who had just inherited a large sum of money — several hundred thousand dollars. When they visited my office and asked how to invest their money for the maximum return, it was apparent that these folks were not from an affluent background.

"You need to be very conservative and preserve your capital instead of spending the money," I cautioned them.

Most people do not get the chance for more than one large cash infusion in their lives. That is why I caution new beneficiaries not to spend all the money on a home or other property but to preserve the capital and let it work, earning interest, and then they can use the interest to buy the things they want.

There are two kinds of people: those who earn interest, and those who pay it.

"I suggest you invest this money and live on the earnings," I advised this couple.

They agreed to invest about one third of the inheritance money with our firm.

"We're not sure how we want to invest the rest. But as soon as we make a decision, we'll get back to you," they promised.

"Are you sure that's what you want to do?" I asked, feeling uneasy about the situation.

After several weeks, these folks phoned.

"What did you do with our money?" they inquired.

Feeling that something could be amiss, I replied, "Tell me where you live, and I'll drive over. Then we can discuss your investment portfolio in person."

As I drove into a lower-class neighborhood, I said aloud, "I can't believe people with that much money live in this part of town."

Checking the address again to be sure, I parked in front of a row of rundown, two-story apartments. To my surprise, a brand new Mercedes and a new Porsche sat in the driveway.

I knocked on the door and was greeted by the gentleman and his wife. As I entered the house, I noticed that the furniture was lavish and loud.

Unable to hide my shock, I blurted out, "What are you going to do with the rest of the money?"

Looking sheepishly at his wife, the husband mumbled, "We don't have any more money."

"What did you do with it?" I asked incredulously.

They had purchased a new boat and a motorcycle, taken a long trip, loaned some to relatives, and bought these new cars. They had blown $450,000!

Dismayed and feeling sick, I drove back to my office. After discussing the matter with a colleague, I said, "I'm going to tie up the remaining money, so they can't get their hands on it."

"That's a pretty risky decision," he warned.

"I know, but I have discretion over the account, and it's the only way to keep these people from spending what's left."

*People who work hard and earn their money develop skills to handle it wisely.*

Sure enough, they were on the phone badgering me to let them get to the money immediately. Although it wasn't easy, I stood my ground.

Today those people are grateful.

The expensive cars wore out, and very little money was recouped from them. The boat was sold for less than half what they paid for it. During the ensuing years, while they were learning to become more responsible, their account grew until they were able to live comfortably off the interest.

## Wealth Abuse

Being financially responsible isn't a product of having wealth. If a poor man suddenly becomes rich, he doesn't become an over-night money master. Being born "into" money doesn't assure responsible handling either. I have seen many spoiled rich kids squander their parents' inheritances and wealth because they couldn't handle money.

Then how does one become financially responsible ?

From my experience, one principle stands out: People who work hard and earn their money develop the virtue to handle it wisely. Most people who have risen by hard knocks know more about how to preserve their wealth than those who get rich quick or inherit money.

The vast amount of wealth in the United States makes money more easily accessible than it is to people living in less-privileged countries. The more substance one has, however, the greater the temptation for abuse. That is exactly what has gone wrong in America: the abundance of wealth has spoiled our thinking. We are affluent as a country, but we have not handled our prosperity well.

I am not against wealth, nor do I believe in a communal or socialistic system. I believe in the free market economy and freedom for everyone in business. I want the rich to be rich because they create jobs. At the same time, I also understand that in the midst of the most affluent nation in world history, many families are suffering because they have abused their blessings. Instead of enjoying America's freedoms, many are bogged down with frustration.

## "So Goes the Nation"

All my life I have heard the saying, "So goes the family, so goes the nation." This is so true.

Several years ago, Americans learned that some of our senators and representatives in Congress didn't even know how to balance their personal and official checking accounts. As a result, they had no idea how much money they were spending. Over-drafting done by our elected officials left the congressional banking system in a shambles.

That same philosophy of spending without accountability has transferred itself into every avenue of our government. Just because Washington is packed with smart lawyers and elected officials doesn't mean they are financially functional. In fact, the opposite is true, as evidenced by the federal government's out-of-control spending that has created our burdensome tax laws and the current recession.

Government, however, merely reflects the values of the public they represent. We gripe and complain about the way our leaders run the economy and waste our tax dollars, but where do our elected officials have their roots? They, like you and me, are products of America's families, schools, churches, colleges, cities, towns, farms, and businesses.

Our elected officials are people, and people have problems. Elected officials simply magnify the troubles of everyday life because they are in the public eye. Every weakness and fault is magnified by the media — especially when money is involved.

Whether you are the President of the United States or the White House butler, it still takes discipline and training to know how to function financially.

Financial woes, moral failures, marriage break-ups, drug addictions in fact, the same social and economic problems found at the grassroots level — affect our elected officials because they drag their difficulties into the limelight with them. It would take too long to list even the most recent departures from Washington whose personal problems forced them either out of office or seriously undermined their credibility.

Most notably, several come to mind like Congressman Rostenkowski, Senator Packwood of Oregon, and Washington Mayor Marion Barry. Many others have gone the way of the wind because of their lack of moral and financial discipline.

Remember ABSCAM? Senators and Congressmen were set up

by the FBI who posed as rich Arabs giving bribes in return for certain favors. The congressmen and senators became traitors and essentially sold out their country for money.

We have even had a president or two — and some very dubious vice presidents — whose moral character and financial mismanagement have affected their political careers.

No stratum of society is immune to the social plagues that could eventually destroy our nation. What causes these plagues? At the root is parental neglect in the home and educational failure in our schools. Irresponsible fathers without the guts to stick around force their children to be supported by welfare and raised in day care centers as mothers are forced into the marketplace. At the same time, our public schools refuse to teach responsibility and accountability, preferring instead to manipulate America's children to further the socialistic goals of educational bureaucrats.

## The Old-Fashioned Way

What makes the family and, ultimately, every phase of leadership in our society dysfunctional? I recognize two key elements that are at the root of America's social ills: commitment and planning.

Lack of commitment has wreaked havoc in this country. Marriages fall apart, people don't care about their neighbors, and everyone is out to one-up the other guy. We have a nation of ingrates living on welfare and other "entitlements."

I don't care how hard it is to do. If you say you are going to be something or do something, then be it and do it!

The American dream used to require hard work and, like Smith-Barney — doing it the "old-fashioned way," by earning it! Not so with most Americans today. Their dream is to have something for nothing with no input and no commitment to do what it takes to become a respectable citizen.

No wonder families break up, kid's rebel, students assault teachers, fathers abuse children, mothers desert their families, and girls abort their babies. Why should we be surprised that Americans are addicted to drugs, alcohol, pain pills, depression medicines, cigarettes, pornography, and violence?

My subject is finances, but all these issues are relative. How can we function financially when our moral condition has depleted our ambition, sabotaged our goals, and waylaid our prosperity?

What made our country strong in its early days? People worked on farms and in the factories. Working made the country fruitful. Everybody worked because if they didn't, they didn't eat. Since there was no welfare or other such free assistance, people got jobs and worked to provide for their families.

Growing up, I worked on a farm. I learned how to plow, bail hay, put tobacco in the barn, and plant seed to grow crops. I also learned a lot about life doing farm work. Although it was hard, I loved it because eventually the crops we planted grew out of the ground. We harvested when the time was right and then were able to sustain ourselves with the products we had worked hard to grow.

> *"When you get where you're going, where will you be?"*

My father also owned a construction company. Today when I visit my homctown, I enjoy seeing the happy people living in the homes we took part in building.

How did I learn to do farm chores and build houses? My family taught me. We worked together, played together, and went to church together as a family.

As kids, we never threatened to blow up the school (oh, we thought about it) or challenged those in authority; we feared our teachers and parents instead of the other way around.

What made America great? A commitment to working hard, caring for our families, and concern for the community as a whole.

## Where Are You Going?

The other key element missing in the lives of many Americans is planning. Someone has said: If you fail to plan, you plan to fail.

Whenever I needed to fill a position in my firm, I started the job interview by asking the potential employee, "When you get where you're going, where will you be?"

That loaded question often results in some soul searching answers. It always amazes me how many intelligent, college educated young people have no clue where they are going or what they are going to do when they get there.

In my business, we required every person who had a top position in our company to do an annual Management by Objective plan. I also use this same management theory in the church where I am executive pastor. This plan asks the person to write a letter to me describing their current job. Then, each executive must list seven or eight goals or objectives he or she will try to accomplish in the coming year. Next, we want to know what criteria he or she will implement to reach these goals.

First, the letter tells the boss whether that person understands his or her job. It may indicate that the employee is in the wrong position.

Second, the goals are important because many times the employee doesn't have goals because he or she doesn't know what goals are. A person who doesn't have even a few, simple goals cannot accomplish anything. Many people go through life this way.

### No goals, no purpose, no prosperity.

Third, the criteria telling how these goals will be implemented indicates whether a person has unrealistic objectives or not. I have had brokers say they are going to get $10 million under management in the next few months but don't have a clue about how to reach that goal. The same has applied to personnel-managing areas of the church.

This may seem like "busyness," but, I can tell you from experience, that goal setting is fundamental to success in life. Why? Because the "pressure cooker syndrome" results from aimless wandering with no clear path or direction in life.

Why live life just going from Point A to Point B, no matter who you trample along the way? Life is more meaningful than that. Poor planning will devastate your relationships and destroy you.

When most Americans want to buy something, they don't care what it costs. They have only one concern: Can it be financed, and what is the monthly payment?

No consideration is given to the fact that the automobile financed for 84 months will be paid for twice over and nothing will be left at the end of the seven years except rust. Why do you think dealers advertise cars at $199, $299, $399 per month? The interest rate may be 19%. But no one cares. "I can afford the monthly payment," the gullible consumer says. Instead of avoiding the pressure cooker, Americans are ignorantly jumping right into the pot. The best way to not get burned is to stay out of the kitchen. Planning ahead to pay for that car — or vacation, or furniture, or golf clubs — will insulate you from the financial fire.

## Handling Everyday Life

How can America's social, moral, and financial problems be solved? Do we have to become old-fashioned or archaic to enjoy peace and prosperity? No. The solution is not complicated. We simply need to do two things: Be committed and plan for the future.

America is the greatest country on the earth, and there are thousands of untapped opportunities available here. Every year new demands create the need for innovative ideas. Each year thousands of dreamers see their dreams come true.

*Be committed and plan for the future.*

This is America, the land of opportunity. What determines who will successfully tap into this vast resource of plenty? One simple criterion: how we handle ourselves in everyday life. I want to provide that in a small way through this book. My goal is to help you find yourself and get into a financial position that will allow you to (1) enjoy life and (2) take advantage of some unique opportunity that may come your way.

When you get where you are going, where will you be? Will you be laughing and singing, or will you be crying? Will you be enjoying the sweet bliss of proper planning for your later years, or will you be in poverty and misery? Your future is being determined by you — right now.

To know where I am going when I am traveling, I must have a map (or a GPS display). I also need a time frame for getting from Point A to Point B, so I develop an ETA (Estimated Time of Arrival).

If I am going home to Kentucky, I call my mom and family and tell them I will be there at a certain time. I can only do this because I have thought it out, looked at the map, and decided how long the trip is and how much time it will take to get there.

If I just start out by happenstance, I may never arrive at all or arrive too late to spend any time enjoying myself. Life is no different.

## To "Get a Life," Have a Plan.

To avoid being boiled alive in the financial pressure cooker, get your life goals and priorities in order.

Planning to build a house? Know how much money it will take beforehand. Looking to buy a car? Find out all the costs involved and then settle on one you can afford.

You may remember the television news program, "Issues and Answers," which aired on the ABC television network from 1960 to 1981.

In all the years I watched it, I don't believe I ever heard the commentators discuss the issue of financial failure as a cause of severe problems on a national level. Why? Because no one dreamed our American families would get into the financial dilemmas they now face.

We must remember that many of the years this showed aired, easy money and credit cards did not exist as we know them now. They could not have guessed that, with so much added convenience, an oxymoron would ensue where the easier life got, the harder it became.

Don't get me wrong. I don't want to return to the days when I couldn't get money out of an ATM machine. Like you, I want the conveniences of life. At the same time, I am advocating that we work hard, earn our own way, and pull together.

I wish I could say I have avoided all the financial pitfalls and potholes that await the unsuspecting and inexperienced; but like many of you, I had to learn the hard way.

When my dad used to tell his friends that my mother put me in the pressure cooker because she had no incubator, he had no idea how much this analogy would apply to my future financial life.

## CHAPTER TWO

# EVERYTHING I NEEDED TO KNOW
# I LEARNED IN BUSINESS MATH

Until the early part of this century, most children were taught a trade. If their father was a carpenter, they learned how to build. If their mother was a seamstress, they learned to sew. Why? Because parents knew that in order for their children to make a living in life, they had to have a marketable skill.

Even today, parents who own a small business often employ their children. I get excited when the landscaper or window cleaner shows up and has his son working alongside him. It thrills me to talk with a client who tells me his children have an active part in the family business. In fact, one of my greatest joys was having my two sons on the staff of my investment firm.

One of the most demanding family businesses is farming. Farm boys and girls learn from an early age what it means to get up before dawn and do their chores before going to school.

Some kids grow up hating farming and never work on the family farm. They realize that farming is not what they want to do with their lives. That is an important lesson. In fact, that is a better lesson than never learning anything, which happens to a lot of children today.

I grew up working on farms part of the time and working in

our family construction business most of the time. Although I didn't particularly enjoy the tasks, I learned the meaning of work. I loved going to my grandfather's farm and helping with the chores and crops.

Later, when I went into the family construction business in another city, I discovered it was not my forte. I quickly shied away from the business as soon as I found another career.

Learning to adjust to the pressures of life is the secret to success. For children who receive no training, adjusting becomes difficult if not impossible, and many times they are condemned to financial failure.

As I examine every area of life, I find that teaching and training is essential. Proper upbringing is the essence of life. To become financially functional, however, we must understand what causes this kind of dysfunction in the first place.

All of us face problems and stresses in life. An adult who has not been properly prepared to meet these pressures, however, will self-destruct like an overblown balloon. Only those who have been taught how to handle common problems can adjust to accommodate the internal and external strains of life.

Three areas of society determine whether a child will grow up to be functional or dysfunctional in the area of handling finances — the home, the school, the church.

## Who is to Blame?

Parents teach children what we want them to learn. Most families are very diligent about instructing kids in proper manners, good sportsmanship, and what is right and wrong. When it comes to teaching children how to function financially, however, many parents fail to pass on the valuable lessons they have learned about money. In many homes, there is little or no financial training given to the children. When I left home at age 18 and went to college to start my life alone, I was destined to face challenges for which I was improperly prepared. Life is full of financial potholes, and I believe I fell into every one of them. Why? Because I was not taught how to function financially.

Although we weren't rich, my father was a great provider, and we had most of what we wanted or at least needed. Growing up, I learned to work and had skills other kids didn't have. I was driving a car by age 10 and, at age 15, could lay concrete, build a foundation, or plant a crop. By the time I was through high school, I could operate almost any kind of farm machinery or construction equipment. I learned skills.

What my father didn't teach me, however, was how to handle the money I would earn from those skills. Since he was very diligent at handling his money, Dad probably assumed that I was watching closely and learning by example. I was watching, but I didn't know how he arrived at his decisions because I — like most kids — was never included in them. I must admit that while my kids were growing up, I too failed by rarely teaching them anything about money. I left that up to the schools, which also was a mistake. As a result, my sons have had to learn, as I did, from the school of hard knocks.

Fortunately, however, my career took a turn early enough for me to help them. For several years while I was in practice, my boys, Scott and Shawn, who are now financial advisors who each earned the right to practice by graduating from college and passing the required federal exams, worked with me in the business because they learned to love it.

## Two Scenarios

By the time my nephew and niece, the children of my oldest sister Linda, were married with children and well into their working careers, they owned their own homes, had savings accounts, autos, and good jobs.

On the other hand, I have seen families with children the same age and under the same circumstances, who couldn't

*What made the difference in these two scenarios?*

afford to pay rent and make car payments, much less have their own homes by the time they reached their mid-20s. My sister's kids did this without help from mom and dad.

My sister made sure her children saved money. When they were small and earned money, Linda taught them to put some of it in a piggy bank. When they received allowances or birthday cash, she would not let them spend the money foolishly or "blow" it. Some of it had to be saved; while the rest could be spent to buy special items that they wanted. Although my sister and her husband could afford almost anything their kids desired, they didn't give in. Instead, they taught Tim and Lee to buy things for themselves with money they had earned and saved.

I can think of countless families who do the opposite. The kids are given anything they want and are spoiled into thinking that the things in life are always going to be handed to them.

Other children are the victims of parents who are so dysfunctional themselves that they become disoriented and confused when it comes to handling money. Some parents even teach their children to "get anything you can from whomever you can get it." As a result, many of these kids turn to crime just to deal with the peer pressure from their friends.

After years of lecturing on this subject throughout the country, I have learned a lot about financial dysfunction in my interviews and counseling with hundreds of people. Kids who function well financially have parents who taught them what it means to delay self-gratification and exercise discipline in handling money,

Out-of-control people who overindulge themselves are like drunken sailors who have never learned moderation. They simply don't know how. Children raised in a happy-go-lucky, eat-drink-and-be-merry environment will find themselves steaming in the "pressure cooker of life" financially, going from paycheck to paycheck as they struggle to keep their heads above water.

Many parents can't teach their children how to handle money properly because they are unable to function financially themselves. How can you teach your children about finances when the kids are well aware of your spending habits and constantly hear you and your spouse argue about money?

## Is There a Solution? Yes.

First of all, it is never too late. Go to the bookstore and buy a book that teaches the basics of household budgeting, balancing a checkbook, and simple financial management. Learn the principles yourself and then teach them to the kids.

There are many practical resources that can be found in the business section of a bookstore, library, or on the Internet, just make sure it is a reliable source

A "Changing America" begins in the home. As the home goes, so goes the nation. This is the starting point. It took generations to get where we are today in America, so the fix won't come overnight.

If everyone would pay attention to this one area of life, then perhaps we could overcome the consumer debt crisis facing our country. As a result, our homes would be more stable and more families would stay together. Maybe we could become an affluent society that would be generous instead of materialistic. It could happen.

## Everything I Needed to Know

By the time I finished fourth grade, I had learned the basics of arithmetic. I could add, subtract, multiply, divide. Even by the end of the third grade, most of us knew the multiplication tables like the backs of our hands. When our teachers flashed those cards in front of us, we made instant response with the answers. We learned to divide by long division. By the fifth and sixth grades, we had learned the short method that cut the division process in half.

These basic arithmetic skills learned in elementary school would come in handy the rest of our lives. In fact, in many instances, they are everything we need to know about math.

During the ninth grade, I failed to grasp the concepts of algebra and was placed into a business math class — a course designed to help us math-challenged kids advance to the tenth grade. Although business math can also be difficult, the basics I learned in that class have remained with me to this day.

In my sophomore year, reality set in. To pass a college entrance exam, my classmates and I were told we needed more advanced subjects like physics, chemistry, algebra, plane and solid geometry, and, in some cases, advanced math courses.

The next three years were a tremendous struggle for me. I failed one algebra course and was finally thrown out of chemistry. Forget physics. During this traumatic time, my sensitive nature allowed me to log in some observations that have remained with me. I am just now voicing them.

My teachers didn't recognize that I excelled in business math but couldn't get the concepts involved in more analytical math. Kids who were whizzes at algebra, however, were failing in English and language classes. I was making straight As in English and took four languages during the course of one year — completing Latin 1,2; Spanish 1,2,3; and German 1,2,3; which was the background that later allowed me to excel in Portuguese, Greek, and Hebrew. I was miles ahead of other kids who were struggling with statistics and problem solving.

## Back to Basics

In college English class, my professor told us that more English majors are in business for themselves than business majors are in business for themselves. That thought stuck with me. Today, my English skills are put to use writing books about financial management!

I had a friend in college who was great at crunching numbers but couldn't spell. Today kids who graduate from high school can do logarithms but can't balance a checkbook. In fact, 95 percent of the math that high school kids learn will never be used the rest of their lives.

I am not advocating that we stop teaching algebra and advanced math courses. We need those subjects, but we also need sound training in basic financial matters like the kind I received in my business math class.

Today, I have a Ph.D. in Business Management, which is one of the most difficult doctoral programs to master. More than half of my education earning an MBA and a doctoral degree required learning to write and decipher extremely difficult calculations.

I am also a financial and investment advisor, which means I must be able to calculate bond yields, calculate straddles, and debit and credit spreads if my client is investing in certain stock options. In addition, the difficult skill of executing hedge strategies had to be mastered to pass exams that qualified me for this profession.

How did I learn those skills? By reading books and taking college classes. Why did I attune myself to such a strenuous degree of study? Because I understood that to make it in the investment profession I had to master these subjects.

In high school, I didn't know what I wanted to do. In fact, I was half way through life before I completed the formal education that prepared me for my vocation as a financial advisor and investment firm owner.

The argument could be made that if I had not been forced to take difficult math courses in high school, I would have failed the college entrance exam; therefore, I wouldn't have the background necessary for the difficult education ahead of me. While this is true, it is not the point I am trying to make.

We need to change the college entrance exams and the requirements in high school and teach our kids more practical subjects that will be useful to them in life. Not every kid is going to end up being a doctor, Certified Public Accountant, engineer, or other such occupations that require advanced math skills.

## Health Class and Home Economics

If I could change one thing about our education system, it would be this. I would require every student who graduates from high school to take one year of Business Math whether they like it or not. In this class, they would learn to function financially. The basic rules of how to run a home and business would be taught. I would also include case studies showing how people should react in given situations as the inevitable pressure cooker heats up.

Why not prepare kids for real life and then add other courses to their studies that are relevant to their chosen career?

Remember health class? I hated health class, but I had to take it. Today, I see the value of that class. In my day, we didn't have AIDS and never had heard of HIV, but we did know about syphilis and gonorrhea. We were trained in personal physical hygiene that made our lives cleaner and healthier. We were also taught how to dress properly. In fact, I learned how to tie a tie in health class!

Today, proper attire is thought to be square, and students dress for school as if every day were Halloween. Kids carry guns, belong to gangs, and buy drugs in the restrooms. Health class is now gender-mixed sex education that borders on the pornographic. Students carrying the AIDS virus are protected, and condoms are distributed in the classroom.

Forty years of liberal-minded educators and elected officials have brought us to this point today. If our schools continue to be undisciplined breeding grounds for sex, violence, and socialism, America will be destroyed.

What is the answer? We need to revamp our entire education system. My intention is not to take on all the social problems festering in our schools today. My subject is finances, but my point is still the same. Unless we teach our kids how to function properly in life, we doom them to failure.

Practical teaching in basic economics is just as important in life as learning to tie a tie, wash and iron clothes, cook, or make a birdhouse in seventh-grade shop class. If parents failed to teach these life basics at home, at least kids could learn them at school.

Instead of helping, our failed education system continues to fuel the moral and financial crisis we face in America today.

## Covering All the Bases

Every year I speak in dozens of churches where I deliver the same message I am trying to drive home in this book. Many times I start my lectures like this:

"I hope you pay attention to me this morning because if someone had come to my church when I was a young man in high school or college or when I was first married, and spent just 40 minutes with me like I am going to spend with you, and taught me the same principles I am going to teach you, it would have changed my entire life."

That got their attention!

When I have been lecturing at a college or university, inevitably a student will walk up to me and say, "Dr. Smith, you don't know me, but you came to my church and spoke to our congregation one Sunday morning. I want you to know I have put into practice the things I learned from you, and it has made a difference right here in college."

After one of my family based seminars, a young married couple told me their parents bought several money management books, got the family together, and they all learned point by point how to function financially. The couple testified they are now much better at handling money because of this last effort made by their parents.

I do not have time in three 40-minute sessions at a university, business luncheon, convention, or church to give all the teaching needed for people to learn how to function financially. I simply try to get the message across that we need to do something about our passiveness in this area.

The churches of America are a very valuable force in the lives of American families and individuals. Churches have significant influence over the education system as well as within politics. Socially, most American communities cannot function without their local churches.

On the weekend, I like to scan the activities page of the local newspaper to see what is going on in the city. An entire section of the paper is devoted to events taking place at the churches in town. A recent sampling included: a divorce support group, drug rehabilitation programs, a family care seminar, and marriage study sessions. These local churches were responding to the needs of almost every phase of life.

One glaring social issue, however, is missing from the church's agenda. In the area of coping financially and training in-home finances, churches are strangely silent. I have yet to pick up my local paper and read about any church having a qualified individual speak or initiate a program that helps people function financially.

When I am visiting a city and lecturing over the weekend, only on rare occasions has the church where I am speaking previously had a financial expert address the congregation. A few times I have discovered a church that has a program in place to help the people function financially. All the bases seem covered, except this one.

## The Business of the Church

Why are many churches strapped for cash and forced to resort to arm-strapping the congregation for money? Because only 25 percent of the people give 95 percent of the money to the church, which pays the bills and maintains the respective ministries; the remaining 75 percent merely volunteer their presence, enjoying a free ride on the coattails of the givers.

I'm going out on a limb with this next statement, but it needs to be said. I don't blame the congregation. They aren't greedy and tightfisted people. Perhaps most are even true Christians. When they can't function financially, however, they have no money left to give to the church.

Most churches encourage tithing, which is giving 10 percent of your income to the church. Almost every denomination teaches this Biblical principle. In fact, this is the financial premise on which most churches base their economic condition.

> *Failing to promote good financial management within the congregation hurts not only the people but also the church.*

It is not my place to prove or disprove the matter of giving to the church — whether it's the tithe or whatever means the church uses to collect money. If, however, the parishioners or church members don't have any excess money, it is very difficult for them to make charity part of their weekly checking disbursements.

Religion and worship are part of America's heritage and culture, and churches are made up of people. As a result, whatever social problems afflict our nation at any given time gets dragged into the churches. That means all the marital and family problems that result from financial failure — or the other way around — affect the churches, making it part of their job to try and help solve the current crises they face.

## Without a Clue

Why are the churches failing to teach financial responsibility to their congregations? I'm in trouble here again because I believe it is the colleges and seminaries who train our young ministers.

In many Christian colleges and universities, there is zero training for future ministers on how to help their church families run their personal economy. The seminaries are very diligent about teaching the soon-to-be pastors how to do a church bulletin, build a Sunday school, and preach a sermon. Young pastors, however, arrive at local congregations without a clue about how to administrate the business of the church.

There are exceptions of course. Many larger and well-organized churches are quite proficient at managing the church's finances, but they represent a minuscule percentage of the churches across America.

In Dr. Elmer Towns' book, *The Ten Largest Churches in America*, he states that the average congregation is only 86 members. That means there are thousands and thousands of small churches in this country.

From my experience, it seems the more conservative churches have the most difficult time with financial management. Why? Most of the ministers of fundamental congregations have attended small, independent church-sponsored schools that do not have accredited courses and are not recognized by any higher institutions of learning. Many are improperly educated even in the areas of Theology and Bible languages, but they graduate as "doctors" from diploma mills that hand out such degrees. Most are unearned.

How do I know? Because as a once fundamental preacher myself, I deal with these people every day in my investment advisory business. Most pastors of small churches have no retirement program or any prospect for a healthy and prosperous golden age. These ministers, most of whom have given up everything for the sake of the ministry, are poor and needy with few resources and usually no savings.

How can the minister teach his congregation to function financially when he does not function financially himself?

This is not a virtue they are trying to maintain. Most ministers I know have given their lives to the ministry but are less than satisfied with the compensation they receive for the unending hours they put into their work. For that I blame the members of the churches they serve.

The churches of America need to get involved with financial teaching at the same intensity they attune themselves to the other issues that plague our society.

## Money - A Moral Issue?

The social ills of our nation are not all financial. At the same time, most of America's social problems are intertwined with the burdens caused by personal money mismanagement.

Why do people sell drugs? To earn money to buy more drugs or to increase their personal lifestyles. Most of the members of the rich drug cartel are worlds apart from the junkies on whom they prey. The drug problem can be traced to a money problem.

Why do people steal? For money. People commit murder for money, lie for money, cheat for money, and commit other heinous crimes too numerous to mention — and for what? For money.

Someone once said to me, "Money really isn't important to me."

> *Money is neither immoral nor moral, righteous or unrighteous. It is how money is used that makes it a moral issue.*

Oh yeah? How about not going to work tomorrow morning, and we will see what money means to you. Everything revolves around money, and that is why it is so important.

No other era in the history of the world has been more reliant upon money than the societies of the late 1900s. Without money to purchase the things we need, it is impossible to survive for very long.

Greed, however, is another matter. Throughout history men have been obsessed with the making and spending of money: Judas Iscariot betrayed Jesus for money; Benedict Arnold sold out the Revolutionaries for money. Some of the most notorious gangsters in history were Americans. In fact, most crimes are committed to get money.

It is not my intention to say that money is immoral. Money is neither immoral nor moral, righteous or unrighteous; it is how money is used that makes it a moral issue.

## What is America Worth?

I do not lose sleep at night for fear of an economic collapse. Bad decisions by policy makers create bad economic conditions. The same policy makers who make the bad decisions, however, can make good ones.

Plenty of people in this nation function perfectly well financially and can bring economic stability to the country. As Americans, we know how to run our business, and we do it better than any nation in the world. We have built the most powerful and successful free nation in history.

My confidence in American resiliency swings my mood away from the fear of economic collapse to a buoyancy of optimism in American entrepreneurship. The creativeness of Americans will ensure our safety for generations.

My concern is that too many Americans are missing the opportunities afforded them because of their apathy toward their personal financial conditions. In other words, things could be better.

We want to give our kids a chance to own part of the wealth instead of becoming part of a two-class society, in which a controlling elite dictates every economic decision. Unfortunately, that is exactly what is happening to our nation at the present.

It is true there are more millionaires and billionaires in this country than ever before in America's history. It is true that no real pockets of extreme poverty exist en masse in this nation. We are wealthy.

One of my good friends, Gary Moore, a financial advisor in Sarasota, Florida, phoned me after reading my first book. In fact, we met through that phone call. Gary made a profound observation that I have heard him use many times to defend America's economic conditions. He says, "Everyone is worried about the debt, but no one seems to talk about how much America is worth."

America does have trillions in deficit spending. Some say it is approaching 8 trillion dollars — some say even more, but that is speculation. Few people realize, however, that our nation's assets total nearly 100 times our deficit or more (actually no one really knows what that figure is). Consider those figures for a moment. If you have $300 trillion in assets and owe $3 trillion in debt, are you bankrupt? I don't think so.

My concern is not the federal deficit but how to maintain and help others take part in the opportunities afforded by America's great wealth.

## Shake Ups and Downsizing

Why do most businesses start and succeed? Because of necessity. That is the number one reason people start a business — to provide income for themselves and their families. In fact, nothing sparks ingenuity and entrepreneurship like the pressure cooker of losing the security of a nine-to-five job.

A friend of mine, Darcie Tabor, of Stamford, Connecticut, worked for an advertising agency until her job was terminated, and she was literally dumped on the street. Young, with no money and a bleak future, Darcie didn't know what to do.

She could have thrown up her hands and sunk into deep depression, but she didn't. Instead, Darcie decided this was the time to act and turn the negatives into positives. Using her creativity, she designed an attractive brochure, mailed it to hundreds of businesses, and followed up with phone calls. Soon a small business was born in Darcie's basement. Today, she operates one of the most prestigious graphic arts studios in the country.

When my literary agent got fired after a shake up at his publishing company, he didn't know what to do. Having never been on his own or accountable for paying his own salary, he found the thought of going into business for himself frightening.

After a long conversation one afternoon, I convinced him to jump into business and create his own job security. As a result, he started his own publishing company. Dave Thomas of Wendy's Restaurant fame became one of my agent's first clients and Mr. Thomas's bestselling book, *Well Done*, was born.

One of the most entrepreneurial principles in the Bible comes from this well-known quote from Jesus, "Ask, and it will be given to you; seek, and you will find; knock, and it will be opened to you." We don't think of this as business advice, but it fits.

Although Jesus was speaking of the initiative we must take in developing a relationship with God, these same steps of asking, seeking, and knocking are the key to success in any endeavor we undertake.

## Something from Nothing

There are literally thousands of success stories in this country from people who have made it to financial security after being almost boiled alive in the pressure cooker. My favorite is the story of Andrew Risso who started something from virtually nothing. (See "Money from Nothing," Inc. Magazine, 1995.)

In 1982, a friend of Andrew Risso's told him about a hospital that needed to buy an energy management system. Risso knew absolutely nothing about energy management systems and very little about electronics in general. Hardly the person who would be interested in installing such a complicated system, Risso convinced his friend to set up the appointment with the hospital administrator anyway.

When Andrew arrived, he toured the facility with the administrator. After the tour was finished, the administrator asked Risso, "Can you suggest anything that will solve our problems?"

Realizing he was in a potential trap and could be found out, Risso countered with his own questions, making them as technical as possible.

"What size are the motors that run the equipment?" he asked. The administrator, who knew nothing about the mechanical side of the equipment, asked Risso to put together a proposal and set up another appointment.

Now Andrew Risso must come up with a company, quick. He grabbed the yellow pages and phoned more than 30 hospitals asking them what type management system they used and would recommend. In only a day and a half, he had settled on the equipment the competing hospitals felt were best.

Risso then called that company and asked if a representative could come and help him make a presentation. This particular manufacturer wanted to get more of their equipment into area hospitals, so they were more than happy to help Andy out.

The presentation was so clear and precise that the hospital administrator turned over the blueprints of the hospital and made the agreement for the new system on the spot!

Energy Consortium, Inc., was born and is now number 316 on the list of Inc.'s Top 500 Companies in America. Andrew Risso wasn't lucky; he was broke, pressured, and smart. He began his company with no knowledge, no experience, no money, and channeled nothing into something.

Opportunities exist in this nation, and becoming a product of its wealth takes more than being a prodigy of luck. Besides, we make our own luck (if you believe in luck). Someone has said, "Luck is when preparedness and opportunity meet one another."

Robert Shook writes books about entrepreneurs — little people who became big people and big people who are still little known because their stories never became public.

It is not my intention to write a book about the stories of entrepreneurs but suffice it to say that opportunities exist in this country, and we are at work because of the ingenious risk taking of giants of the past. I could fill a book just from the vision of one man, Benjamin Franklin, whose inventions in the 1700s are still changing our world. The recession that hit the country in late 2007 has created thousands of opportunities because of necessity. Sometimes adversity is the greatest creator.

## Avoiding the Big Blow Up

The changes needed to turn this country around will take dozens of years, but we can do it. First, we must get serious about adjusting to the more complicated structure of life that progress has brought us.

The entire key to economic stability lies in education. We start at home; we change the public educational system; we educate at church.

In the end, when the country gets back on its feet, gains a handle on its financial situations and starts functioning properly, we will realize that the changes begun at the grass-roots level have achieved their purpose.

Those little boys and girls who grow up in the future will govern this country like our forefathers intended. They will make good, solid decisions that will affect all of mankind, and they will do it because they received the right teaching about how to function financially while they were young.

You, however, are probably at the point in your life where the financial pressure cooker is already heating up. Otherwise, you wouldn't be reading this book. Just because the fire is hot doesn't mean the pot has to explode. You can still regulate the flame and escape with your financial health in tact.

Many people are afraid to use a pressure cooker because of stories they have heard about Grandma's chicken gumbo exploding into a giant mess on the kitchen ceiling. The problem is not with the pressure cooker but with the person responsible for regulating the flame under it. When used properly, pressure cookers can produce tender, steamed meat in a way no other appliance can. The key is keeping the temperature under control.

During a lifetime, we all end up in the financial pressure cooker at one time or another. What will be fanning the flames? The fear and anxiety that accompanies every kind of money problem.

The loss of a job can turn a confident corporate executive into a defeated drunk if he sees no hope for the future. A loving marriage can become a nightmare if one spouse refuses to control his or her spending. A lingering and expensive illness can ruin a family's security if there is no health insurance.

The death of a loved one can be overwhelming but even more painful if the funeral has to be financed; more disastrous if the widow or family is left with loads of debt; more stressful if the surviving spouse doesn't have enough income after the family provider has passed on.

The pressure and stress caused by the absence or abuse of money has taken its toll on thousands of people, but it doesn't have to be that way.

In the chapters that follow, I provide practical steps to defuse the potential for financial disaster. For those who are presently simmering in the pressure cooker of a financial crisis, I will help you identify the dysfunctional financial lifestyle and suggest ways to defuse the stress it causes.

Let's face it — these are not pleasant topics. Retreating into denial will only make matters worse. Now is the time to lower the temperature — before the pot is out of control and blows up in your face.

# CHAPTER THREE

# THE DYSFUNCTIONAL FINANCIAL LIFESTYLE

What is the source of most financial dysfunctionality? Debt. Let me make it clear that I do not consider debt to be a negative issue. Why? Because credit can be used as leverage to the advantage both of the one who gives it, and the one who receives it.

In my book, *Exploding the Doomsday Money Myths*, I take on the doomsayers who are proponents that all debt is bad and no one should ever have any. As well, they go beyond what is truth and speculate that debt is non Biblical. A person who believes this is not only naive but is completely out of touch with what the Bible has to say about these matters.

Our entire economic system runs on credit. Businesses start up and thrive because of credit, and the stock and bond markets run on it. Saying there should be no credit or debt is ridiculous. In fact, the complicated bartering system that involves credit actually keeps America alive and flourishing.

On the other hand, as much as credit is a blessing, it can also be a curse. Most entrepreneurs who have blossomed into billionaires have used credit to the greatest advantage. Those who end up in bankruptcy court or financially destitute are usually there because they have abused credit.

Whatever the outcome, most of us have taken on some debt by the time we are out of high school. If we escape debt in our high school years, most of us have some debt by the time we finish college or get married. In fact, many marriages start out with some degree of debt.

Most college degrees could not be earned without some debt being incurred by either students or their parents. Student loans were designed to make it easier for students to get through college and get an education necessary to survive in today's world.

To expand, many businesses sell off bonds, which are debt securities to investors. Or they may leverage from the bank to expand their services, which means hiring more employees. This creates jobs for all of us.

## When Debt Becomes a Problem

Debt becomes a problem when spending gets out of control. As a result, the business, family, or individual starts to sink financially.

In his book, *Your Money: Frustration or Freedom,* author Howard L. Dayton includes a quote from Franklin D. Roosevelt, who said in 1932, "Any government, like any family, can for a year spend a little more than it earns, but you and I know that a continuance of that habit means the poorhouse."

When debt can't be repaid, creditors start calling, and the pressure begins. Many creditors are ruthless. If they find you won't pay up, they will turn you over to a collection agency that will pursue you like a wolf after a sick lamb. I know people who have committed suicide or ended up in the hospital because of the ruthless pursuit of creditors.

I recently had a person call me in the vicinity of where I live. I did not know that person, but her story was heart wrenching. She was a victim of terrible abuse by her husband. After weathering these storms, she kicked the bum out and tried to function; but found the debt he had incurred in her name so large that she couldn't manage it.

With tears flowing she said to me, "The calls I am getting from creditors about debts I didn't even know I had are causing the most anxiety I have ever had."

I have never been one to waste words, so I said to this lovely lady, "You look terrible; you are obviously under a huge load of stress. You need to get into the hospital."

"I have no health insurance and no money for doctors," she replied.

This story ended in a tragic case of suicide. In her parting letter, she said that the threats of creditors to financially destroy her, and the embarrassment of liens, bank levees, and such drove her to this final escape.

Although this story is extreme, I have wondered if the attitude of collection agencies and attorneys–that everyone who doesn't pay is a deadbeat–has caused innocent people to jump off the bridge. It is true that people get very ill who are put under this kind of pressure. This is one reason I am a firm believer in bankruptcy for the right reasons.

Some people borrow money from their family members, friends, or relatives. If you think bill collectors are relentless, try reneging on a debt owed to your uncle!

Most credit problems do not happen overnight. They develop over long periods of time as our lifestyles change. Sometimes they come so slowly that it is undetectable just how much debt has accumulated. Then one morning, you wake up and find yourself in the depths of despair because you can't pay your bills.

Howard L. Dayton says it like this: "The modern American is a person who drives a bank-financed car over a bond-financed highway on credit-card gas to open a charge account at a department store, so he can fill his savings and loan-financed home with installment-purchased furniture."

I can add that he goes to a bond or bank-financed church on Sunday to confess the sin of it all!

Someone once jokingly said, "The cost of living is the difference between your net income and your gross habits."

Borrowing is the normal way of life for millions of Americans. Most of us cannot live without borrowing. Many, however, have borrowed their way into oblivion and simply cannot manage the debt they have accrued. Others borrow, pay it back, borrow, and pay it back.

Certain types of people should never go into debt. On the other hand, others could responsibly take on more debt. Their diverse lifestyles and control each will or will not exercise over their priorities makes the difference.

## Killer or Convenience?

At one time, I worked with the woman who had a hand in inventing the credit card. Day after day, Vi Winsloe traipsed up and down the steps of the Chase Manhattan Bank trying to sell bankers on the concept of a card that would give consumers instant credit. I remember when credit cards didn't exist, but imagine trying to get along without one now.

Certain people should never be given a credit card. Others have many credit cards in their wallets and purses but know how to handle them.

According to a Wall Street Journal article titled, *Credit Cards Aren't a Hazard for Everyone,* more and more people are using Visa, MasterCard, Discover, American Express, and ATM debit cards in place of cash and checks.

Some folks have become "chronic convenience users" and are often proud of the fact they charge everything from milk and eggs to dental cleanings. Then they pay their credit card tabs in full when the bills come each month.

What are the advantages of such disciplined financial habits? *Savings in Time and Money* makes this comment: "Compared with people who pay cash," this article notes, "convenience users make fewer trips to the automated teller machines or ATMs. They fuss with fewer bills. They get no-cost loans for an average of 45 days by taking advantage of interest-free grace periods on their purchases."

In fact, more than half of all spending on Visa and MasterCard credit cards is by convenience users. Being a spender and not a borrower also allows you to hang onto the money for an extra few weeks and pay fewer ATM fees.

This practice, however, still requires diligent money management and essential record keeping. One way to do this is to record each credit-card charge in your bank account register as if it were a cash withdrawal. That way you will have enough money to cover the balance for that month.

Who shouldn't use credit cards for convenience spending? Anyone who already has a balance on one or more cards for a month or longer. This statistic applies to nearly 75 percent of all card holders. If you do have a revolving balance, then you cannot take advantage of the free grace period, and you may end up paying interest of 18 percent or higher.

Guns do not kill people; the person who pulls the trigger kills people. Likewise, a credit card is not evil in itself; it is the person doing the charging who makes it a dangerous weapon. Learn to use credit to your advantage and avoid the temptation to overspend simply because you can say, "Charge it."

## Slick Advertising

While in San Francisco recently, I spotted a homeless person squatting on the sidewalk watching a battery-operated color television set. In the United States, 95 percent of the people have television sets and most of them are in color.

In the mid-1950s, color television did not exist in our neighborhood, and my family didn't even own a TV of any kind. In fact, there was not even a television station in our area.

It was in the mid '50s before our family got our first phone. We had four-digit numbers and a huge party line; we thought we were in tall cotton. Little did we know that 40 years later we would be able to call the farmhouse from a cellular phone while riding on the tractor!

It is now possible to walk through a steamy, primitive jungle somewhere along the equator and talk to your party anywhere in the world. In fact, a missionary friend of mine emailed me from his phone, and he was on a nearly unexplored river in the State of Acre, Brazil. He and I had traveled that river with a paddle and pole when we were teenagers; then there were zero communication possibilities in that part of the world. At present, AT&T has the technology Craig McCaw invented hanging on a satellite orbiting the earth. Phone wires will soon be nonexistent because all phones will be cellular.

What does all this have to do with financial pressure? Plenty. So many technological changes have occurred in recent years, it is impossible to list even a trifle of them. Every year they make our gadgets better. Every year the media blitzes our households with advertising on the changes. It is quite possible that you are reading this book on the new Kindle Technology that someday may replace books as we now read them. What do these blitzes create? It puts the pressure on us to buy the products they are making.

We are bombarded by the media with easy credit and convenient terms. If you think you don't need something, it doesn't matter; the pressure to buy will be so great you'll buy it anyway.

All our homes are filled with stuff we don't need. We trade cars instead of fixing them up, and we upgrade our lifestyles taking on more responsibility all the time. It is the American way of life.

John McArthur, in his book, *God's Plan for Giving,* writes, "The American way is to buy things you don't need with money you don't have."

You can finance anything today. I heard a comedian tell about a guy who financed his tattoo. Imagine the consequences if he missed a payment. The tattoo would be repossessed!

I love the game of golf and play it regularly. It is the way I relax and the way I take my vacations. At times, I am obsessed with it.

In golf there is a stroke of play called a "drive." The drive is very important because it is the first shot and must be hit on the longer holes with a club called a "driver," which is the number one club in the bag.

Since I have trouble at times hitting with the "driver," I have six of them in my locker. Why? Because I am a victim of slick advertising. Every time they make a new driver, and Phil Mickelson or Tiger Woods tells me their new driver can fix my slice or hook, I buy one. It is all media hype. A good salesman sold me on a new pair of golf shoes because Tiger Woods wears them, and he swore Tiger said they add 15 yards to his drives. I'm wearing them.

Today golf clubs have special colors and certain aesthetics to make them look as if you can play scratch golf with the pros. The truth is, I can hit my 1965 Wilson Staff clubs almost as well as I can the four sets of clubs I now own trying to improve my game. By the way, purchase a set of Callaways —they not only look good, they work (I think).

Furniture ads tell you, "Buy now, and don't make any payments until June of 2012!"

Once while visiting my dad in Kentucky, he wanted to check out a big screen TV set — you know, "a monster" complete with whistles and bells.

We arrived at the store, and there stood the biggest TV I had ever seen. A huge yellow sign screamed, **"I CAN BE YOURS FOR A SMALL MONTHLY PAYMENT!"** In small print, the awesome, long-range terms were spelled out.

*No one could afford to buy that thing, including my father,* I thought.

"You're not going to spend that much money on a television set and then finance it to boot are you?" I asked in dismay as I saw my dad's eyes light up and his hand reach for his wallet.

"That's my business," he responded nudging me out of his way.

"Your mom and me, well, we don't see so good anymore," he explained with all seriousness. "Our eyesight is failing, not to mention our hearing."

"Dad," I exclaimed, "You could sit across the street without your glasses and view that thing!"

My objections were to no avail. He died happy. He and my mom owned two giant televisions complete with DVDs and a satellite dish!

All the media hype and advertising pressure can cause the most resolute among us to crumble and yield to the desires we had previously been nurturing only in our minds.

### Like a Bird?

Remember when you used to look forward to getting your paycheck every Friday? You had accomplished something and were proud to receive your wages. Now, the gleam that was once in your eye is gone because you never see your money anymore. You have become a mailing service for your creditors.

> *We are no longer living to work; we are working to live.*

Can you remember when you used to love your job? You looked forward to going to work. Now, there are so many things to pay for that working is no longer a labor of love but a chore that must be performed every day.

This was graphically illustrated to me one day while sitting in my office looking out the window. I noticed a bird flying in the sky.

This particular day I was sort of melancholy because of troubling issues going on in my life. I thought, "Man, I would love to be a bird. All you do is fly around all day looking down on the world, instead of the world looking down on you. You have nothing to do but fly around heaven all day with no worries, no frustrations, and no troubles like I have now."

Then the bird landed on the ground where it began foraging for a worm. All the while, the tiny fowl kept one ear to the ground listening carefully for any approaching prey, but it also had one wary eye spying on the cat lurking on the fence above it.

That cat had one thing on its mind: to eat the bird. It promptly did.

As the cat scurried away with feathers protruding from its lips, I remember thinking, "God, I don't want to be a bird! Birds don't live; they just exist."

This is what financial pressure will do to you. It will suck the life out of you, making you unable to function properly. You have one eye on the plow tilling the ground to grow your food while the other eye is on the creditor perched on the fence ready to devour you.

## Are You Over-Extended?

One of the most popular topics I have ever written lists the "28 Ways to Know You Are Overextended." This list has been published in many periodicals, newspapers, and magazines around the world. I use it in my seminars and include it here to help you determine if you are sinking into the financial pit of overextension.

Take this test by answering Yes or No to the following 28 statements:

1. *You don't know how much debt you have and are afraid to add it up.*
2. *You pay monthly bills with money targeted for other obligations.*
3. *You pay the minimum payment on your credit cards each month.*
4. *You increase your credit limits on your credit cards.*
5. *You increase the number of your credit cards.*
6. *You pay off credit card payments with other credit cards.*

7. *You write post-dated checks on a regular basis.*

8. *You spend money in advance of pay day and must hurry to the bank on pay day to cover the check2s you have written.*

9. *You often have a negative balance in your checkbook.*

10. *You receive regular overdraft notices from the bank.*

11. *You only pay the interest on bank loans.*

12. *You increase your borrowing limits at the bank.*

13. *You don't have a savings plan.*

14. *You cannot live three to six months without regular weekly or monthly income.*

15. *You decrease your 401k or pension contribution at work.*

16. *Your mortgage payment or rent is more than 45 percent of your monthly take- home pay.*

17. *You are one or more months behind in paying one or more bills.*

18. *You are behind in paying all your bills.*

19. *You use savings for household needs.*

20. *You cancel auto insurance on one or more cars.*

21. *You cancel your health insurance.*

22. *You pay for regular household bills with borrowed money.*

23. *You borrow money from an uncommon source to pay bills.*

24. *You have received a letter from a collection agency.*

25. *You have had something repossessed.*

26. *You have a pending judgment that cannot be paid.*

27. *You are considering bankruptcy.*

28. *You are paying your bills with money normally given as tithes and offerings.*

If you answered "No" to five or fewer questions, then you have sound money habits.

If you have 6-10 negative responses, then you need to watch what you are doing and make some minor changes to improve your situation.

If you have 11-15 negative responses, then you must take immediate steps to rectify the situation because you are in trouble. I call it "running uphill in a mud slide." You are probably surviving, but going backwards.

A score of 16 plus means you must do something quickly and are probably headed for bankruptcy or you are already there.

## The Rich and Famous

What is one sure way to overextend your finances and end up in the pressure cooker? Trying to emulate the lifestyles of the rich and famous.

There used to be a television program called *Lifestyles of the Rich and Famous*. It was hosted by Robin Leach. I hated that show. Watching people who live in a world we can't fathom can be depressing. For most of us, it will be impossible in this life to live on such a grand scale. You need to accept that fact. If you don't, you can create a lot of stress for yourself. Some people never realize their incapability to become rich and famous.

Too many Americans are chasing a pot of gold at the end of the rainbow. Doing this will drive you into an unrealistic fantasy world. The desire to be rich is a deadly trap, and Americans fall for it more than any culture on the earth. We must have everything and at all costs.

Some families are destroyed by materialism. Fathers and mothers are working two and three jobs trying "to keep up with the Joneses" so that every whim and desire will be satisfied. Instead, all they do is sink deeper and deeper into dissatisfaction.

Almost everyone envies rich people; even rich people envy rich people, and that drives them to strive to be richer. The envy of the rich can cause emotional problems. No wonder one of the Ten Commandments is, "Do not covet."

This was graphically illustrated to me Christmas morning in 1986. We had recently moved from Kentucky to Northern California so I could finish certain educational requirements and work at a new job. Just before Christmas that year, the family wanted to go back home to visit the grandparents for the holidays.

Knowing they were homesick, I insisted they go. Circumstances with my work prevented me from joining them. This would be the first time in my life I had not been with my parents and family for Christmas.

Somewhat depressed on Christmas Eve, I decided to get away

from the house at least for Christmas Day. I had heard that Beverly Hills is beautiful at Christmas time, and having nothing else to do, the notion of going somewhere new was alluring to me. Besides, for most of my life, I had longed to visit Beverly Hills because it was the home of most of the stars I had watched on TV and seen in the movies for years upon years.

## Bummed Out in Beverly Hills

I had recently purchased my first BMW and wanted the opportunity to see how it would perform on a long road trip. I packed for a couple of days and drove the 500 miles to Beverly Hills, arriving late that night.

Upon coming into Beverly Hills, the city was fascinating. The decorations were unlike any I had ever seen in any town anywhere I had traveled in the world. The huge homes were delightful. Rodeo Drive was everything I had imagined it would be.

I arose early on Christmas morning and drove into the residential area of Beverly Hills. I could not believe the beauty of the area or the sizes of the homes. They were huge. This was a great time to visit because there was virtually no one on the streets or the freeway. Los Angeles traffic can be brutal on most days, but not on Christmas Day.

I made my way up and down the streets gawking at everything that moved. Using a tourist map, I picked out the stars' homes and waited, hoping to catch a glimpse of someone famous. Sure enough, Ed McMahon came out of his house and got into his car. Well, he wasn't Charlton Heston or Clint Eastwood, but he was famous.

Beverly Hills is very hilly, but its name decries the real description. It should have been named Beverly Mountains. Most of its steep streets wind around hair pin curves.

As I rounded a curve and was pulling a steep hill, I approached a van from the rear. For some reason, the van had stopped on the hillside. Since there was no room to pass, I had to wait until the driver got the vehicle started, so he could move on up the hill and out of my way.

To my amazement, the van suddenly started rolling back down the hill toward my new car. Not being too familiar with my new

BMW, I had trouble finding the horn button. In my panic, I couldn't get the car in reverse either.

With no way out, and the driver apparently unaware I was even back there, the hitch on the van's rear slammed into my BMW. The force of the impact moved my car 30 to 40 feet down the hill.

Both the driver of the van and I got out and surveyed the damage. I was inoperable. After some conversation with the van owner, who was a German student from New York in California for vacation, I decided to call the police. The young man admitted the accident was his fault and was willing to wait until the police arrived.

I needed a phone, so I started toward one of the houses. Trying to enter a resident's home in this rich town is impossible. No one would let a stranger inside even if he were the President of the United States.

The first house I came to had a big gate with a stiff warning to keep off the premises. The second house had the sign "Beware of Dogs."

Below the warning stood two Doberman Pinschers drooling like they hadn't had their regular choice cut steaks for a few days.

I could not get close to knocking on the door of one of these houses. Finally, after about an hour, a garage door rose and revealed a nicely dressed lady getting ready to leave. I called out to her and asked if she could call the police. She said she would, so I returned to my car.

When I arrived back down the hill where the accident had taken place, to my amazement the van had vanished without a trace. I had the license plate number, but to this day neither the driver nor the vehicle was ever found. If that guy is reading this book, give yourself up.

As I stared at the front of my car, two patrol cars of the famous Beverly Hills Police Department arrived. Hoping to get them hot on the van's trail, I was shocked when one of the cops said, "We can't do anything for you. You will have to call your insurance company because there are no injuries."

"But what about hit and run?" I exclaimed.

"Sorry," they said, they drove away leaving me distressed.

Oh, they did call a tow truck.

## Gloom, Despair, and Agony

While I was sitting in my car waiting for the tow truck, I began to look around. It suddenly dawned on me that I was in one of the richest areas of the world. These people had plenty of money.

I began to reason with myself. "My insurance bill is going up. I can't afford this wreck. I have to pay $1,000 deductible before the insurance company pays a dime. This isn't fair."

Before long I had sunk into such depression, despair, and anger over the situation that I was starting to blame all the rich people in Beverly Hills.

I thought, *They don't have these kinds of troubles because they are rich. If they did get in a wreck, they would just pull out one of their other Mercedes and never miss a beat.*

I began to get bitter because I felt the whole incident was an unnecessary blow life had dealt me. This feeling is not unlike one that many others have felt at times of financial stress in their lives.

Have you ever driven through the rich neighborhood of your city on a day when you are having trouble paying your bills? When you glance up at the mansions, have you ever thought how unfair life is?

Asaph, the song writer, had the same problem. In the Book of Psalms, Chapter 73, he wrote, "For I was envious at the foolish for there are no bands in their death: but their strength is firm. They are not in trouble as other men: neither are they plagued like other men, their eyes stand out with fatness: they have more than heart could wish (KJV)."

Apparently Asaph had a bone to pick with rich people.

Materialism causes all kinds of stress. Jealousy and envy are heart-wrenching emotions. When we are not satisfied with who we are, what we are, and where we are, we are in deep trouble.

Sometimes we feel if we had a lot of money, life would be a piece of cake. Money does make life easier, and having enough of it is something most of us never enjoy, but would like to.

Someone said to me one time, "Money is not the number one thing in my life, but it is way ahead of number two."

The real truth is money doesn't have the intrinsic value of being able to bring happiness.

Since that day in Beverly Hills, I have matured a little, and I understand that rich people have the same stress and trouble I experience. Although they might not have them in the same way, suffering is suffering and stress is stress.

Our American society is too focused on the material things of this world. It dictates everything we do. We have embraced several ideals that have given us the wrong attitude about money. Let's see how this has affected us financially.

## Shoppers or Savers?

In a Forbes magazine article titled *Hey Big Saver,* the author, Janet Novack, points out that some Americans appear to be oddballs because they want to save money.

More people, however, are putting money into retirement, and today they have more to contribute because of the new forms of tax-deferred programs such as 401(k)s, Roth IRAs, and other forms of tax-sheltered investments.

Although there seems to be a swaying away from consumption, America is still a nation of shoppers. There have been very few Christmas seasons when shopping records have not been broken.

We invent ways to make shopping more convenient. Sears had no sooner suspended its Roebuck catalogue when the shopping-by-mail experience resurged. In my opinion, Sears missed the boat again.

Specialized magazines now come by mail, and you can order all kinds of odd little items that you had once thought about and wished you had invented. Today, shopping by television and on the Internet is becoming increasingly popular. In 2009, when this book finally came to a conclusion, almost anything imaginable can be bought on the Internet. Alaskan Governor Sarah Palin even sold the state's jet on eBay.com.

> *Postponing gratification is always the best policy.*

Most Americans operate under this philosophy: "Get as much as you can now and worry about paying for it later." Instant gratification, however, carries a heavy price tag.

Most young people, as soon as they graduate from high school or college and get a job, go into debt for an expensive new car. They don't realize they will be paying for an automobile the rest of their lives.

When I am speaking to college crowds, I tell them what I would not do if I had life to live over again. I would not spend my money on fancy cars. I would be much richer if I hadn't done that. Instead of buying a brand new Dodge Hemi four-wheel super truck with the big tires and paying half my salary each month to have it, I would have socked the money away in the bank.

Why? Because of the wonder and power of compound interest.

If you invest $100 per month at 10 percent and start when you are age 20 and do it faithfully each month, you can stop when you are age 28 and never add another dime to your account the rest of your life. When you are age 65 years old, you will have $494,000.00 in your account. If you annuitize the same amount, it could be as much as $532,000.00.

If you start at age 28, then you must put away $163 per month until you are age 65 to reach the same goal. The figures are staggering the older you get. If you are age 52 and want to start, forget it.

I have had many of my friends ask me to illustrate this to their children because it is a graphic example of the difference between where most people are headed and where they could be headed. I regularly give this simple illustration in churches, schools, and colleges where I speak, and I know this one small addition of knowledge has made a difference in many young people's lives. I believe in saving, and the Bible teaches it. I sometimes teach economics for a week at our private Christian school. Many of those young people have savings accounts because of the conviction this kind of teaching brings.

What would all of us have done if we knew this secret at age 18? Would we have bought that new car, or more expensive home, at age 28?

Many have asked me just how to get 10%; increasingly so during this recession of 2009, which will go down in history as one of the most brutal. This is accomplished fairly easily, but not in this market. You can barely get 2% in a money market, and forget investing in anything else.

So how can this be accomplished?

My book published in 1997, Put Your Money Where Your Heart Is, gives the ins and outs of investing and shows how you can earn more with your investment dollars without taking a lot of risks. This recession will end and the markets will right themselves from bottom up. The key is to invest and stay put, do dollar-cost averaging, and maintain discipline. Over the length of your life, with good solid advice, you should be able to average this amount without much risk. There could be some years when the rewards will be much greater, which will offset a sure downturn in the future, and the average yields will allow you to complete your investment goals.

## Novelty Versus Value

Perhaps you are reading this book, and you don't consider yourself to be wasteful or materialistic. I suggest you tour your garage, basement, or attic and take inventory of the things you once had to have but now no longer need. You will be astonished at how much money you have wasted on worthless goods.

Material things are nice, but if you cannot afford them, then it is an illusion to think they will give you a better life.

More than 50 percent of American homes now have a computer. Unfortunately, most of these computers are used for playing games. Some are used for legitimate purposes, but very few.

Through advertising, computer companies have convinced us to upgrade every time they come out with a new product. Having a super-fast computer today is equivalent to yesteryear's men wanting the baddest-of-big engines in their cars. Do we really need supercharged computers to run a simple household budget? The truth is it takes more RAM to run the computer games.

*Novelty in technology often takes precedence over good sense.*

I used to sell adding machines for Remington Rand. In 1966, they came out with a calculator that ran through a cycle and would add, subtract, multiply, and divide automatically. After completing the process, which took several minutes, the machine then spit the calculations onto the paper roll. At the time, Model 104 was the state of the art calculator.

Seven years later, the first LED calculator came on the market. This fascinating little machine could be held in your hand and add, subtract, multiply, and divide instantly. I had to have one, so I paid $80 in 1973 for a calculator I can now buy for $3; one that also can do square root, percentage, and has a memory.

Remember how much you paid for your first computer? It is now so obsolete you wouldn't bother using it — in spite of the fact you have upgraded it many times. Computers that cost $2,500 in 1995 are now $450. The same equipment you are paying large amounts of money for today will cost far less in the future.

Cellular phones, telephones, televisions, radios, clocks, and virtually every new-fangled electronic gadget will gobble up your dollars if you get sucked into the trap of upgrading your toys.

So, what's my point?

Evaluate the necessity of what you are buying before you buy it. I am not advocating we stop purchasing the latest technology, but I suggest doing so only if it actually enhances our lifestyle instead of merely draining your wallet and cluttering your closets.

## The Dysfunctional Financial Lifestyle

We choke the financial life out of our being by trying to keep up with everybody else. Americans have the attitude today that the right watches, cars, pens, and clothes make us more acceptable to others, and we spend a great deal of money trying to arrive at a status most of us can ill afford.

Why have we gotten to this point? Because of the dauntless effort of advertisers. Millions fall into their cleverly devised traps everyday.

In the book, *Mind Over Money,* authors Wayne Nance and Dr. Ed Charlesworth explain how advertisers sabotage American households: "A dysfunctional financial lifestyle is an addictive and malignant pattern of consumption, purchasing, spending, or deferred payment plans." They go on to say that advertisers target "intelligence, morals, and personality, based on preconscious beliefs that: designer, highly visible, or advertised items yield satisfaction. The most technologically advanced version of fax, beeper, mobile phone, stereo, or large screen television reflects that we have made it and are therefore worthwhile.

If our income does not keep pace with our desires, we should tranquilize our anxious dysphoria with the American drug of choice and follow the wisdom of the great leaders of our deficit-spending society to charge our way out of despair."

I support all the wonderful things that make our lives better. What I am against is junk. And I'm just like you; I have plenty of it. Our fascination for junk is the psychological response put into our minds by advertisers who want to get their sticky fingers into our bank accounts or on our charge cards.

I want to see Americans enjoy their lives and be emotionally fit at the same time. I do not want to see this country so debt strapped because of being caught up in a make believe world that they cannot function properly. I want to see the social problems relating from financial difficulties eliminated - and that can come through basic education.

On the other hand, I believe every citizen should achieve his or her full potential in this great land of opportunity. I realize the benefits of charge cards, automobile loans, and long-term mortgages. I consider credit to be a great tool that, used properly, can enhance our lifestyles.

As for the debt-free proponents, they are out of touch with the real world. To justify their paranoia, they want to make everyone else miserable.

We don't live in a third world country where having things in advance and being able to pay them off over time is a non-existent pipe dream.

Americans should take advantage of every opportunity we have at our fingertips to better ourselves.

## When Outgo Exceeds Income, Upkeep Will Be Your Downfall

My goal is to teach a balance between consumption and savings. The economic term for this is "Consumer Equilibrium." This is what you and I need to attain. The balance between what we take in as income and what we can spend to maintain a certain lifestyle needs to be in focus.

Someone said it so brilliantly, "When your outgo exceeds your income, your upkeep will be your downfall."

I want to help in a small way to relieve the stress that financial pressure causes by attacking the root of the problems.

The business owner who determines the amount of his employees' incomes has the same problems as the man who goes to work and collects a paycheck every week.

Businesses go broke every day — and that hurts all Americans. Why?

Because businesses create jobs, and jobs relieve unemployment, which relieves financial stress on our entire nation. I often wonder if those same businesses that went bankrupt would still be operating today if one change concerning the management of their money had been instituted.

Be careful who you envy. I have been shocked many times to discover that someone whom I thought didn't have a care in the world was actually in deep financial trouble.

## Making "Rich" a Relative Term

Ask yourself: "Do I *really* want to be rich?"

We live in a capitalistic society, and the concept of capitalism dictates to us the thought that we ought to be rich. There is nothing wrong with this notion, unless you are avowed to poverty because of your religious beliefs or socioeconomic convictions.

There is a certain obsession with the idea that poverty is awful, deplorable, and dishonorable. In some cases it is. The fear of poverty can send the average American into deep depression. At that point, poverty becomes a sin and being rich appears to hold all the answers to life's most perplexing dilemmas.

On the other hand, I know people who "hit it big" after years of living in poverty, and then felt guilty because of their newfound wealth. They won't frolic in their riches because friends and family get left behind when the wealth separates them socially.

It is just as perplexing for a person who lives in rigid and austere discipline concerning excessive materialism. That person judges the rich and tends to want to make the wealthy conform to his set of standards — standards, by the way, that are impossible to keep.

A missionary client of mine once visited my offices in Napa Valley, California. His reaction to our Victorian building, which is an old house beautifully remodeled into office space, and the size and expense of our automobiles was one of disgust.

"I could not personally spend that kind of money on material goods when I have seen so much poverty throughout the world," he said.

This is a noble opinion, and my first response would be that I too care about the poor, but that doesn't mean I should avow myself to it. There isn't one of those in dire need who wouldn't trade places with me.

In the second place, people with disgust for riches must fully set the example. If and when those who propagate that wealth is a misdemeanor, if not a felony, should divest themselves of virtually everything they have and live by example. The question then becomes "How much is too much?"

And therein lays the trap.

Most missionaries and other non-profit workers are supported by the gifts and donations of people who have adequate resources and a willingness to share some of their wealth. Because of others' generosity, these workers can fulfill their calling and life-long ambitions.

> **People who become rich sometimes wish they weren't.**

My mentor, Adam Smith, and his philosophy have had a profound impact on the way I think. In Smith's *Money Game* — the best book ever written about money — he makes this thought-provoking statement: "The love of money as a possession — as distinguished from the love of money as a means to the enjoyments and realities of life — will be recognized for what it is, a somewhat disgusting morbidity, one of those semi-criminal, semi-pathological propensities which one hands over with a shudder to the specialists in mental disease."

Greed creates the emotional desire; guilt causes the stress. The poor and desperate can be just as greedy as the rich. Both try to take from the other. Think about it. The love of money causes both these problems — and that is what makes people financially dysfunctional. If your financial condition dictates your emotional stability, then you are dysfunctional when it comes to money. You can be rich — or poor — and still be financially dysfunctional. Why? Because you have allowed your financial position or your possessions to determine who you are as a person.

Worry and stress are highlights of a life with some bumps. Knowing how to handle your finances is one way to ensure that functional stability will give you a peaceful life.

## CHAPTER FOUR

# DEFUSING FINANCIAL STRESS

What is the main cause of financial stress? Fear. I am not a psychologist, but I have spent countless hours counseling with people suffering from the tremendous pressure that builds from being afraid of the unknown. People under severe financial stress can come to the point of lost sleep, changed eating habits, extreme weight loss, emotional trauma, and family problems – all caused by fear.

Why do we get afraid? Three sources create fear:

1. **An event from the past haunts us.**
2. **The situation in the present upsets us.**
3. **A prediction of the future threatens us.**

Any one of these can cause tremendous pressure in a person's life. Sometimes all three are occurring at once. When that happens, the results can be devastating.

Let's look at these three sources of fear in an effort to relieve or prevent the pressure that financial stress causes.

## The Haunting Past

Many people are paralyzed with fear because of traumatic events that happened in the past.

My parents and grandparents went through the Great Depression. Although my parents lived during the Depression and experienced the effects of it, they were too young to feel the emotional impact of those desperate years. My grandparents, however, never fully recovered from the trauma caused by that difficult time in our nation's history.

My grandfather and grandmother lived on a wheat farm in an area of Ottawa County, Kansas, that was hit hard by not only the Depression but the horrible dust bowl that resulted in four long years of drought.

My grandmother told me, "I can remember standing outside in the hot Kansas wind watching the grasshoppers literally destroy a whole field of crops in a day."

With little grass in the fields, the cows couldn't eat, making milk a rare commodity. Food was scarce, money was sparse, and life was dismal. My grandparents, like millions of people during those horrid years, were very poor.

Before the Depression, my grandfather was an enterprising man — a trait he inherited from my great-grandfather who settled 7,000 acres back in the late 1800s. The old sod houses he built on the Kansas farm estate near Longford, Kansas, still stand today.

My grandfather's thriving farm produced thousands of chickens, dairy cattle, and one of the few large cherry orchards in that part of the country. The land he owned also contained a huge rock quarry from which he supplied gravel for the roads in the county.

Grandpa was at the peak of his financial success when the Great Depression dealt its devastating blows. In the ensuing years, he was barely able to hold on to his farm and merely eked out a living instead of becoming prosperous once again. Immobilized by fear, Grandpa never fully recovered from the pain and misery of his financial loss. Haunting thoughts of the Great Depression kept him from taking any steps toward entrepreneurial endeavors again.

## Hidden Assets

John Steinbeck's classic book, *The Grapes of Wrath,* tells about families much like my grandparents whose livelihood was wiped out by the Depression, forcing them to leave their farms and seek employment anywhere they could. Thousands of Depression refugees migrated from the Midwest to California, where their descendants live today.

In my work as a financial advisor, I have met many of these retired, working-class Depression survivors. Over the years of dealing with these people, I have never met one who was not extremely conservative with finances. Their fear of experiencing another Depression makes it difficult for them to take financial risks of any kind.

Some people are so afraid of economic collapse that they guard every cent and will not place a dime in the bank. They have their money buried or placed in secret vaults.

Remember the movie *It's a Wonderful Life?* Remember the scene where the townspeople crowd into Harry Bailey's Building and Loan to demand their money? Bank collapses during the Great Depression left many people afraid of the government and the banks.

Occasionally, one of our clients would inherit an estate left by an elderly relative. When the heirs go to inspect the property, they discover cash and liquid assets behind picture frames, in walls, under beds, and in other creative hiding places.

When I was a kid growing up in a farming community of Kentucky, an old man lived next door to our little country church. His log house had a dirt floor and no electricity. Living alone for many years, he wore old dirty clothes and eked out a living on his little farm using a mule to plow the garden. Out of kindness, he occasionally mowed the grass in the church cemetery.

One day, someone discovered this old gentleman lying in the cemetery, dead of apparent natural causes. Those removing the body found thousands of musty dollars rolled up in the old man's pockets. Thousands more were retrieved from clever hiding places throughout his house.

That is not an isolated case.

One of my clients inherited a cardboard box from an eccentric old lady who had a small house stuffed with junk. No one would ever have known she owned a cent. In the box were bonds, stocks, and cash worth more than $1 million.

This kind of eccentricity is not limited to senior citizens. One of my clients, who is relatively young, had to be convinced to take her money out of plastic bags in her freezer and put it in the bank where it would really be safe.

## Four Fear Deflators

Fear of another Depression is not limited to those who went through it or who can remember it. Even members of my generation can become paranoid simply by reading or studying about the Great Depression. They are afraid it will happen all over again.

It's no wonder. Americans seem obsessed by the tragedies resulting from that period of our nation's history. Volumes of books have been written concerning the possible collapse of our economy, and the devastation it will cause as everyone loses.

How then should we handle financial fears created by paranoid "experts" who want us to believe in and prepare for another economic collapse, greater than the Great Depression of 1929?

Let me make several suggestions.

### 1. Don't panic.

After years of being brainwashed with the idea that everything will blow up in the end, people have a tendency to react as extremely as the story they are being told. Fear of losing everything is very real to some people. The resulting reaction can tip a person into a drastic financial position and actually unbalance his or her ability to react normally.

Although I recommend caution with a conservative flair, I believe it is unhealthy to sit around worrying about the government collapsing and the banks losing all your money. I can sympathize with people who have been burned financially by someone or something. I know it is hard for them to risk their money in a new venture.

Someone put it this way, "Once you have been run over by a Mack truck, you wait a little bit longer before you pull out into the intersection."

Natural disasters and transportation accidents occur in our country every year, leaving financial and emotional devastation in their wake. Most of us, however, still fly in airplanes, drive on highways, and ride the rails. Americans continue to live and build homes in tornado zones and earthquake-prone areas. Few people pull up stakes in spite of the fact that hurricanes and floods happen along the coasts year after year.

## 2. Study the facts.

Most people who worry about the Great Depression don't know why it happened, nor do they understand it is unlikely to happen again. Why? Because of government safeguards against economic collapse.

Remember when the stock market crashed in 1987? Falling more than 500 points in one day, the 1987 plummet became the greatest single stock market disaster ever — worse than the crash of 1929.

For years, economists had predicted a market crash like that of 1987. How did the economy respond? Three months later, there were no proven adverse effects on the economy. Why? Because of circuit breakers the New York Stock Exchange had in place to prevent an economic collapse.

Another reason our economy remained stable in 1987 related to the fact that we are no longer dependent on the Gold Standard. At the time, the Federal Reserve prudently pumped money into the economy. If America had been on the Gold Standard, the money supply could not have been manipulated because we would have been locked into a fixed commodity —and that would have surely bankrupted us.

Before you panic, get the facts on every issue.

## 3. Beware of doomsayers.

Some authors and advisers who claim to be financial experts aren't experts at all. Before you act on what a so-called expert is predicting, check to see if economic conditions are changing all that much.

Harry Figgie writes in his ominous book, *Bankruptcy 1995, The Coming Collapse of America and How to Stop It:* "In 1995, the United States of America, as we know it today, will cease to exist. That year, the country will have spent itself into a bankruptcy from which there will be no return. What we once called the American Century will end, literally, with the end of the American way of life."

Now there's a cheery thought.

But 1995 has come and gone, and nothing Figgie predicted happened. Mr. Figgie exhibits the extent to which some people, who are fearful of the past resurfacing, will go.

The World Market announced it was going to downgrade the dollar which would have an adverse effect on the American economy. When news that the World Market flexed its muscles, the stock market set a new record!

If you do not get anything else out of this book, learn this: Don't get stressed out because someone has told you the economy is going down the tubes. Even if it did, what could you do about it? If America gets hit by another Great Depression, then everyone else — both rich and poor — will be in the same boat.

If, however, there is something you can do about a given situation to make the road easier then there must be a way out for everyone, and that is exactly my point. What is the best stress reliever? To be doing everything you can to prevent disaster in the future. The rest of the world will take care of itself.

### 4. Get professional advice.

Before you make hasty financial decisions, I suggest you seek out a professional about your particular situation.

You wouldn't ask your next door neighbor for medical attention or suggest your co-workers write a prescription, would you? Why then, when it comes to financial advice, would you take the suggestions of talk show economists who know nothing about your personal finances?

Making investment decisions or changes in your financial status requires a lot of creative thinking and the ability to trust the system to a certain extent. Many people who could be making more money in the stock market today aren't because they were afraid to stick their necks out a little.

Being too conservative is like driving on an interstate at 35 miles an hour; at a nice, easy, slow pace. Even with caution you can get killed just as quickly if someone hits you at breakneck speeds.

Investment professionals make decisions every day based on what has happened in the past. We do pay attention to trends. The way we treat trends, however, keeps us from going into a panic the way a novice would. Investment professionals study trends to avoid threatening situations, whereas non-professionals make fear-based decisions without the proper understanding of how to avoid the threatening situation.

Your financial health affects almost every other area of your life — from marital to physical. Not paying strict attention to how you invest or use your money can have devastating consequences as you get older.

## The Threatening Present

The second force that creates fear in our lives comes from the state of our current financial situation.

Almost every day, someone asks me for advice about how to bail out of a negative money problem.

During a recession, the calls increase, particularly from people who are connected to some cyclical industry that has been hit hard. Laid off or out of work, they need help adjusting to the present crisis. If they are business people, they have to accommodate when work slows down and sales are flat. Bankruptcies and foreclosures intensify during these harder times.

Sometimes problems arrive without any prior notice. The boss decides he doesn't like you anymore, and suddenly you are fired. Or, a worker receives notice that the plant is shutting down and moving, and you aren't going with it. Congress or the President closes a military base that has kept an entire community alive for almost a century, and the lives of thousands of people are immediately affected.

Unpredictable negative changes can create a lot of tension. Since almost every adverse situation has a financial consequence, I want to illustrate those problems and make suggestions as to how to cope with them or fix them. Let's look at the four most common.

- Health and Physical Problems
- Natural Disasters
- Job loss and/or Unemployment
- Domestic Problems

## Health and Physical Problems

A diagnosis of terminal cancer or some other fatal or debilitating disease can create tremendous psychological and emotional problems.

As the tragic news sets in, other fears emerge. The threat of not being able to work and earn a living, the reality there is not enough money in savings to make the mortgage payments, and the fear that your family will have to live with less after you are gone. Such uncertainties put unnecessary stress on an already anxious patient.

Because of this hypothetical illness, you might be wiped out financially and lose everything because of the way your finances have been handled. Nothing is more devastating than to be thrust into a situation of failing health that threatens your family and your individual security. Unfortunately, it happens every day to thousands of people.

Many times serious health problems cannot be avoided, but the aftershock can. How? By planning.

## Purchase Health Insurance

In today's society, it is financial suicide not to have health insurance — along with enough coverage to take care of catastrophic illnesses. In addition, neglecting to have enough life insurance to cover all of the medical bills that health insurance does not pay straps the family with the unpaid balance.

Have you ever received a bill from a hospital and not paid it? If you have had this experience, then you know firsthand that hospitals are ruthless when it comes to collecting their accounts. They don't care whether your family is starving or not. They will come after you with all the fury of hell to collect the debt. I have seen hospitals garnish wages, knowing that patients will lose their jobs and be unable to pay.

Sure, deadbeats need to be hounded, but honest, hard-working Americans deserve more respect and understanding from hospital collections departments.

In spite of the expense, I personally would not be without health insurance. I would work an extra job to have it no matter what the cost because of the devastating effect not having health insurance could have on my family's future.

## Get Life and Disability Insurance

Leave your family debt free. Term insurance — the only sensible kind to buy — can be very reasonable, making it possible for you to leave your family in good financial shape.

One of the most misunderstood forms of insurance is disability insurance. If you are an independent business person, do not be without it. If the company you work for does not have it, then purchase some for yourself.

Disability insurance is expensive but well worth the cost considering the risk of losing the ability to earn a living. You may live to be 100 years old, but that won't do you much good if you are disabled at age 40 and unable to work. I could give countless examples of acquaintances who are disabled and financially distraught because of it.

In fact, becoming disabled by an accident is more likely than having a health problem. Getting hurt on the job or injured at home or in a car accident creates multiple physical and financial problems. If you get disabled by your own volition, you have no one to sue for the damages.

> ## *Personal insurance against catastrophe is your only way out.*

Several of my clients have been physically mangled in car accidents. One slipped and fell in his bathtub; another fell out of his own tree while building a tree house for his kids. Today, disability payments and their personal savings are the only income they have left. Otherwise, they would be bankrupt and miserable.

The good news is you can avoid the financial pressures caused by severe health problems and disability.

## Natural Disasters

I moved from Kentucky to Napa Valley, California — one of the most beautiful places to live on God's green earth. I fell in love with the Valley the first time I drove through it. *Surely there is no more suitable paradise for one to hang his hat and spend out his days,* I thought, while enjoying the warm sunshine, breathing the smell of fresh grapes, and enjoying the crisp, cool ocean air.

Napa Valley is a veritable Garden of Eden.

At first, it seemed I had found heaven on earth. For months it didn't rain, yet the Valley was cool and green. Every day it was possible to picnic, bike, hike, or golf. Rain was rarely an issue, except from late

December to early March. Even then, it rains mostly at night leaving the days free for outdoor activity. Pure Paradise,

After living in the Valley for a couple of years, I was in for a rude awakening. The rains came — and came and came.

The last time I had seen it rain 25 inches in three and a half days was in Manaus, Brazil, on the Amazon River during my student days! When the equivalent came to California, the ocean could no longer suck up the surface water running into it.

High winds magnified the problem by blowing the tides up the rivers and backing up the water. Beautiful Napa experienced a "200-year flood," so to speak, and the entire area was under water. It was the most water I had ever seen inland in the United States.

A couple of years after the rains, the earthquakes started. I knew about the big one in 1906, but that was a long time ago, and I had been in Napa for several years and never felt a tremor. The threat was overstated, I told myself, and nothing to really worry about.

On October 17, 1989, I was sitting in my den watching the opening five minutes of the third game of the Bay Area World Series. The Oakland A's were playing the San Francisco Giants.

Suddenly the chandeliers started swaying, books began falling, the house was rocking back and forth, and the TV went blank. Water sloshed over the sides of the hot tub, and the dog kept running around in a circle. I ran outside and watched the ground buckle up and down as it rolled like a tidal wave.

Then it was over.

The aftermath of that 7.1 earthquake was not as devastating as it could have been because the usual commuters on the Nimitz Freeway in Oakland, California, were at home watching the World Series on television. Businesses had let out early, and the traffic had cleared before the quake hit.

The unique engineering earned after the 1906 quake kept the downtown San Francisco buildings intact. Only the Marina district, which was built on fill and sand, received major damage.

The next day, I drove to San Francisco to survey the quake's aftermath. Buildings in the marina district had toppled into the street. The entire fourth floor of a condominium high-rise, where a friend of mine lived, lay in ruins on the ground.

Many buildings were still on fire. Sections of the street pavement were sunken as deep as 10 feet. Water was spewing from the hydrants, and the foundations had crumbled underneath the buildings.

Fortunately, the owners of these exclusive homes were high-income people who could afford earthquake insurance. Otherwise, the financial devastation would have done more damage than the earthquake. All in all, only 6 billion dollars of damage was recorded throughout the Bay Area. That is minimal compared to what could have happened.

Other people in the world are not as fortunate. Natural disasters occur all over the globe. People in Asian and African countries are starving because of famine, earthquakes, and violent storms. They are at the mercy of nature and have no recourse against what happens to them.

In the United States, it is different. Floods occur, hurricanes rip through our coastal cities, and tornadoes suck the life out of the ground and buildings as well as take their toll on human life. The problems created by the aftershock of natural disasters are the most serious.

While we can't prevent natural disaster, we can prepare for them. Preparing for financial disaster makes the experience less devastating. Not being prepared is foolishness.

## Purchase Disaster and Fire Insurance

If you live in an area where natural disaster has struck before and could strike again, then you must prepare yourself for it. Insurance, if you can get it, is the best policy.

Fire damage can be devastating. Not having fire insurance is inviting pain and suffering. Losing everything you have in a fire is terrible, but not being able to replace it is even worse.

The loss after a natural disaster can affect your way of living for years to come. While you can never replace keepsakes and a life of memories, you can preserve your lifestyle as you once knew it by preparing financially in case something unfortunate and potentially dangerous occurs.

One stormy night in 1980, a huge bolt of lightning shook our house. Fortunately, the lightning rods I had installed the week before did their job and the house was saved. Without the lightning rods, everything in our house would have been history.

They say lightning never strikes you twice. Wrong. We built a home in the area of the beautiful horse farms in Lexington, Kentucky. The Blue Grass Area, like Napa Valley, is serene, green, and many say more like Ireland than anywhere else in the world. I had flown by myself from our home in Napa Valley to our home in Lexington, Kentucky. A storm had blown up quickly, and as I was on the rural lane that led to my farm, a large bolt of lightning struck in the distance. *I hope that wasn't my house,* I laughed out-loud to myself.

I couldn't raise the garage doors and had to enter the house by the pass door in the basement. I tried to turn on a light, but nothing happened. I realized the electricity was knocked out. I grabbed a flashlight and noticed that the light switches had blackened around the plates. Obviously, the lightning had struck my transformer. This was a geothermal house, so I had my own transformer. I called the electric company, and they came out at 2 a.m. and got the electricity on by replacing the blown transformer. I called my electrician and asked him to stop by the next morning. He said he could be there at 8 a.m.

That night I slept in the great room of the house so that I would not over sleep and miss the electrician. Everything was fine until the next morning at 7 a.m. when my neighbor noticed my house was on fire. I had checked through the house thoroughly, but I could not see behind the rafters in the roof where we had enclosed the attic. The lightning had blown a hole in the roof which was 42 feet in the air, and ignited the fascia board high on the roof. It smoldered until the wind blew through the attic and fanned the flames. My neighbor banged on the window until I woke up and got out of the house before the fumes and smoke had killed me. We both stood there and watched the column of fire shooting through the roof.

The house was saved by 13 pieces of fire equipment, and I can't say enough about the Fayette County, Kentucky Fire Department. Their bravery saved a life-time of treasures and my house. One fireman told me they had less than five minutes left to get the fire out, or they were going to let the house burn to the ground. He asked me what was the most important thing in the house, and he would try to get it. I was on the cell phone with Kathy back in California, and she said, "Get my pictures." I told the fireman where they were and later he came out with a blackened face holding all the albums that preserved our heritage.

The fire made the news on all the TV stations in Lexington and the paper, plus my neighbor no doubt saved my life.

The damage to repair and replace furniture, etc., was nearly $600,000. My life savings were in that house. Had I not had insurance, I would have been penniless. However, the gracious insurance company cancelled my policy, and I was forced to pay a higher premium to insure my home.

Insurance can be your lightning rod. Buy the kind you need and rest easier.

## Move to a Less Disaster-Prone Area

The next best way to avoiding financial ruin from a natural disaster is to move to a safer area.

I have never been able to understand why people continue to clean mud out of their houses when the creek or river floods every few years like clockwork. These people must enjoy swimming in Hepatitis with water up to their eyeballs.

In areas where disasters occur routinely, it is foolish to live in fear and incur the expense of rebuilding every few years. It may be cheaper to sell your home and move than to stay where you are and purchase expensive flood, hurricane, or earthquake insurance.

## Job Loss and/or Unemployment

In San Francisco's Bay Area, where I used to live and work, the closing of military bases in the mid-1990s by the Clinton Administration created havoc in many lives.

I lived near Mare Island Naval Base, which operated from 1859 to 1995. The surrounding towns had thrived for many years, not only from the military presence but also as a result of the prosperity of the civilian population working on Mare Island.

Closing the base not only affected the people who lived and worked in the area, but also the business community that depended upon the income derived from base employees. As a result, the economic survivals of the families who live in the surrounding cities have been dealt a devastating economic blow which is still affecting them as they get hit again by the current 2009 recession.

Many families associated with the defense industry have been uprooted, and generations of tradition have been dismantled. With few new jobs available in the community, many families had to move to unfamiliar territory and start all over again. Those left behind had to adjust to living in a depressed economy where once there had been a thriving community.

Naval base employees who had worked long enough received an early retirement and survived. Others not as fortunate had to seek other means of making a living.

Losing a job can happen to anyone at any time. The problem escalates when the country is in recession. Recessions cause unemployment rates to rise, and the danger of being caught without a monthly income increases.

Many people think their jobs are invincible because of the stability of the company where they are employed. Recent layoffs and downsizing by large companies like AT&T, IBM, Ford, GM, and thousands of others prove no one is safe.

Well-known companies that were once listed on the New York Stock Exchange now no longer exist. In fact, the list constantly shifts as the economy changes. Today, there are no buggy whip manufacturers or horse carriage companies doing business on a grand scale employing thousands of people.

Most Americans at one time or another experience job loss — either because the company goes out of business, downsizes, or undergoes a corporate takeover. In today's recession, the possibility of job loss occurs because industry sales are dropping like rocks, bankruptcies are setting a record, and the unemployment line surges.

## The Myth of Job Security

Job security is a myth. Why? Here are a few reasons:

### 1. Recessions are inevitable.

Industry is related to a sector of the economy that gets hit especially hard during a recession. When recessions come, auto manufacturers lay off thousands of workers and close plants. The construction industry regularly contributes to the unemployment lines when housing starts decrease.

**2. Elections alter the economy.**

When the local, state, or federal government changes hands, tax laws and policies that affect workers in areas dependent on government contracts undergo revision. The defense industry is especially vulnerable at all times.

**3. Change in ownership alters the direction of a company.**

When a business is sold, the new owners may sell off part of the company to raise capital. Many workers get bumped in the reorganization, and jobs are lost.

**4. Administrative changes can create chaos.**

If the new management cannot control the company, financial trouble results and jobs are lost.

Years ago, I worked for Thomson McKinnon Securities. One Friday afternoon, management officials announced the company was going out of business, and 4,000 or more brokers plus thousands of personnel would be let go. We had no previous warning until we were told "to get prepared to be out of work the following Monday."

"I didn't know Thomson was in financial trouble, did you?" asked a shocked co-worker. Apparently, the only ones who had time to prepare were those in top management who knew what was coming.

"Who would have thought a company this big could be facing bankruptcy!" she exclaimed, trying to hold back the tears.

"What am I going to do now?" I asked myself, almost in a panic.

I wasn't alone. The news hit us all right between the eyes. Everything was fine, and then all of a sudden our false sense of security crumbled before our eyes.

## If You Lose Your Job

What can you do if you suddenly lose your job?

**1. Don't get caught.**

Be prepared in advance in case this happens to you. Never rely on anything to be permanent — as thousands of workers discover each year.

**2. Invest in your 401k or 403b plan at work.**

Most businesses have this type of tax-sheltered plan, which is a pretax deductible from your paycheck. Check with your company and see how much you can contribute and then contribute the maximum if you are financially able. When you are fired or dismissed for some reason or other, the investments can be rolled out of the plan into a separate IRA that your financial advisor can manage for you.

Some companies offer profit-sharing plans as well. You will want to participate in any savings vehicles the company offers.

**3. Set up an IRA.**

If your company does not offer a savings plan, then set one up yourself. You can contribute up to $4,000 per year if your spouse works, or $2,200 if he or she does not. Open an IRA and put money into it every month or fund it for the whole year up front. You can deduct this contribution from your income tax.

**4. Get a pre-approved line of credit at the bank.**

Some banks will hold a line of credit for up to 10 years. This can be done as a home equity loan, even though you never use it, or on your signature if you are financially strong enough.

**5. Have enough savings in the bank to ensure three to six months living expenses without any income.**

This will give you enough time to locate another job.

**6. Build relationships with other companies by letting them know your skills.**

Always have a relationship built somewhere else. Oftentimes this is invaluable after the loss of a job.

I have given this advice to people who have had no intention of leaving their jobs but found better and more secure situations than their present place of employment. Others have used this strategy while keeping their present job — until the pink slip came. Because they had paved the way beforehand, they never missed a paycheck.

**7. Have prearranged permission to skip one or two payments on mortgages or personal credit bills in case of an emergency.**

Many credit card companies will let you do this, thereby protecting your credit rating.

The Bible has a great way of explaining how things change. "Kingly crowns are not in the house forever." When the king gets toppled from the throne, his demise affects all the subjects.

The only strategy against job security is to be prepared before you lose it.

## Domestic Problems

The most complicated and financially devastating domestic problem is divorce. We will deal with the financial difficulties created by divorce in a Chapter Five.

## Threatening Future Predicaments

If you are a worrier, then nothing can cause you more grief than events that threaten your future. Although it is a sin to worry, I have probably done more of it than anyone, making me an expert on the matter. However, I have learned to control this habit by realizing worry changes nothing.

When I asked my brother-in-law, Fred, if he ever worries, he replied, "Of course. Worry is necessary. If I worry, I might think of something that will help."

> *Fear of the future can be very real - in spite of the fact nothing bad has happened yet.*

Worry may not be a virtue, but I understand what he means by this statement. When we are threatened, our natural response is to mull ideas over in our minds and actually imagine different scenarios as to how certain situations could possibly work out. If the situation is intense enough, it can affect our eating habits and our emotional stability.

Fear of the future has its roots in every man's quest for materialism. When that desire is dominant, then the compulsion makes us subordinate to being greedy and possessive.

Although I pay little attention to psychologists, I did happen to catch the advice of one man while watching TV one day. He made a good point about how we handle negative thoughts about the future. "Futuristic problems," according to this man, "can only threaten you as far as you are willing to let yourself be threatened." I agree with him.

The future is never reality until it actually happens. Predictions are made based primarily upon what we think might happen, not what actually has happened.

Instead of being afraid of the outcome of a particular situation, we should face the problem in the opposite direction. You can only control the present. Therefore, you can control the future by controlling the present.

If you are afraid you are will be overweight when you reach your 40s or 50s, then you must control your appetite at the present. If you are afraid your health will fail, then you must eat right and stay in shape by exercising throughout your life. A person who has the tendency toward alcoholism can only control the situation by moderation or total abstinence.

Your financial future can be approached in the same way. In 35 years, how much money will you have? How about in 25, 20, 15, 10 or 5 years?

In your lifetime you are going to make a lot of money. Whether or not it will be enough money depends on how well you plan to spend it.

Your financial future deserves your immediate attention. My book, *Put Your Money Where Your Heart Is,* pinpoints where you should be financially. It also gives you expert advice on how to invest your dollars to make the maximum amount of money without undue risks.

Here are a few suggestions you can follow to help you prepare for your future:

1. **Hire a financial planner.** A professional financial planner will be able to give you an overview of where you are financially and where you are going. It is worth the cost because most financial planners will save you enough by suggestions on your tax situation, investments, etc., to pay for their fee.

2. **Save money.** Put some money aside — no matter how little — until you get to the point where your savings each week are

substantial. I suggest you save 10 percent of your income. Pay yourself each pay day. You can do this by participating in your 401k, 403b, or profit-sharing plan at work. These are pretax savings dollars. You pay a lot of other people so why not pay yourself?

**3. Budget.** A lady once said to me, "Don't make me budget. I'll feel like I am in jail. I won't be able to spend money!" I replied, "Madam, a budget will allow you to spend the money you have." A budget is simply a plan for spending money. That's all it is. It doesn't have to be complicated or fancy. It only has to be realistic.

Here is a simple budget plan for you to follow:

35 percent of income for rent or mortgage payments

25 percent for household expenses — food, gas, utilities, etc.

20 percent for lifestyle — eating out, vacations, clothes

10 percent for church

10 percent for savings

You can modify and adjust these percentages at will but do not mess with the church and savings. Banks like no more than 35% of disposable income for a mortgage payment, and most financial advisors agree. I believe you can increase that percentage and decrease something else depending on how important your home is to you. Also, the home is an investment, so an increase of five points or so should not upset the balance between consumption and savings. These are percentages that are safe and have been proven for years.

I have never seen a household or business in financial trouble that had a budget and stuck to it. In spite of the safeguards that a budget provides, I would estimate that 90 percent of the households in America have no idea where they are financially, and most don't even care!

Americans are more concerned about their ability to make the monthly payments on their automobiles than they are about protecting their future.

## How Can My Business Survive a Recession?

Economic cycles cause a change in planning, a shift in thinking so that when the dust settles, there is life after death. Here are some things you can do to protect yourself and help you make sensible decisions during these tough times. If you are attuned to the problems, you will create the answers. I was talking to my long-time partner, Jim Johnson from Reno, the other night and his comment as we were discussing this book was, "There is one sure thing: you will never do business again the way you used to do it."

He is exactly right. The ending of every deep recession we have had in this nation has created changes in the marketplace and new innovations that never existed before. In the last part of this book, I give you an illustration that graphically supports this fact.

Here are some things you can do in your business right now that you may not have already done. One of the things I am advising young people in business is to sell their "toys" and preserve their capital. The kids won't die without RVs, swimming pools, and country club memberships.

1. **Forget your business plan of the past.** Anything you planned previous to this recession is obsolete. You have to adjust accordingly. To spend depending on a budget that worked while you had a strong cash flow will be a waste of time. Make the shift to survival and decrease spending.

2. **Look at your bank account as the last penny you will ever have.** Adjust your spending based upon preserving your capital. Credit is almost non-existent, so this is a paramount discipline to maintain your balance.

3. **Do not take on any more debt.** If you can't pay off the debt you have, you shouldn't be taking on more burden. This will only hasten the demise of your business.

4. **Create alliances with people you want to eventually hire.** Top-notch people may not be available to you because you can't afford them. Start developing relationships now because there will come a time when you will be able to put some of those people to work, assuming your company survives the recession.

5. **Keep your quality at top-shelf levels.** Jack Welsh was named "Manager of the Century" by Forbes Magazine because of his basic philosophy that made General Electric the company it is: Do not depreciate your quality simply because times are hard.

The way your customers are treated will be remembered when everybody else is open for business.

6. **Do not hide the recessionary facts from your employees.** Everyone in my workforce understands times are hard, and we want to keep our favorite people around the shop, so I explain the difficulties and include them in process of survival.

7. **Keep goals realistic.** We use Management by Objective as our model for business management, and we do it religiously. Although complicated at times, the plan is simply objectives you are requiring your management to reach by aligning the work force to get the job done. Each year, we spend an entire day working on these plans. One of the things you cannot do is keep expanding those goals when there is no money to pay for them. This is a formula for disaster. Keep your objectives within reach, and this will keep your employees from being discouraged.

8. **The death spiral will engulf you if you do not act quickly.** I am dealing everyday with businessmen and women in trouble, or who don't want to get into more trouble. It is "Survival of the Toughest." Thousands of businesses are going under every day and there's no end in sight. Whether your business survives will depend on how quickly you can employ means of survival.

## Before It's Too Late

I spend my waking hours talking to and working with people concerned about their financial futures. I suggest ways to invest their money without making decisions for them. Together, we are controlling the future by planning in the present. Nothing makes me sadder than to meet elderly people who are destitute financially. And believe me, there are plenty of them out there.

Many older folks did not plan properly, and in the end are in dire straits. They either have no children to look after them, or their children won't. There is no extra money to travel or to enjoy those things all of us look forward to doing in our old age. What could be more tragic than to work all your life and then come to your golden years and find you can't make ends meet?

Social Security will not provide for all your needs. You must have another source of income to live. You must also consider the possibility that you may not want to or even be able to work until you die.

As farmers in Kansas, my grandfather worked almost up to the day he died at age 90. My grandmother died in the garden hoeing weeds at age 77.

Not all elderly people, however, will stay healthy.

How would my grandparents have fared if they had gotten ill 15 or 20 years earlier and couldn't work? I believe they would have lost everything they owned because they depended upon the income from farming and dairy products until they died.

The expected lifespan of most Americans increases every year. If you are under the age of 65, you will probably live to be 90. That means you will need even more money than if you live to be 79.

With this increase in lifespan, the retirement age will also rise. This is one way the government will keep the Social Security System intact. Unless you are independently wealthy — and most of us are not — you cannot afford to have your head stuck somewhere in the clouds while you pretend everything is going to be all right. You must make sure you have done everything possible to ensure a bright future for yourself and your family.

Fear of financial disaster probably causes as much panic as anything we will ever experience in this life.

Over the years, I have dealt with four major areas of financial difficulty that put people in the pressure cooker. In the following chapters, I will discuss divorce, bankruptcy, retirement, and the IRS - and how you can avoid financial disaster when the heat is on.

# CHAPTER FIVE

## DIVORCE - BEFORE AND AFTER

In 1968, Tammy Wynette came out with the hit song, "D-I-V-O-R-C-E." In this rendition that made her very famous, and probably very rich, she spells out the words that she doesn't want little J-O-E to hear.

Why was this song a big hit not only on the country music charts but on the pop charts as well? Because it focused on the harsh reality of a problem that would eventually plague our nation and, in some way, touch the lives of almost every American.

If something isn't done, our nation's rampant, runaway divorce rate could destroy us. In fact, I believe the single most devastating problem faced by our nation today is the breakdown of the family. Why? Because divorce undermines moral values, creates havoc in the lives of children, frustrates, and sabotages the spiritual values upon which America was founded.

With 55 percent of marriages now ending in divorce and rising, the impact can be felt in every area of our personal, family, business, political, and religious lives. In the pressure cooker of life, divorce is the most volatile, disruptive, and explosive event a person can encounter.

Although I am not a psychologist, much of my education deals with human relations. With a Master of Divinity, I have served churches as associate pastor, senior pastor, and currently as executive pastor. I have settled cases in court and have first-hand experience with divorce. I believe the knowledge of how much stress and suffering that divorce can bring has not been learned by counseling with others as much as from personal experience.

## Not Made in Heaven

Divorce occurs for many reasons, some of which cannot be prevented. It would be naive to think that every marriage is going to work out. Right or wrong, sometimes marriages are not made in heaven. In fact, some are doomed from the start.

When couples get married too young, immaturity and inadequate adjustment create problems that in many cases cannot be resolved. A lack of teaching and counseling early in the marriage leads to permanent damage.

Speaking of failed marriages, my mother once told me: "A failure in the end is the result of a fatal fall in the beginning."

Sacrificial, unselfish love must be present in the beginning for the marriage to survive in the end.

Nevertheless, I do not believe divorce is right. In fact, some of the conflicts over which people divorce could be resolved with proper counseling and training or pure understanding and obedience to Scripture.

If I had it to do over, I would not lay a guilt trip on those considering divorce or who have been divorced. As a pastor, I have changed my thinking entirely. Instead of condemning them as in the past, I try to help them. Ostracizing and condemning divorced people only drives them away from God and prevents them from receiving the support they need during this traumatic time in their lives.

It is easy to condemn and judge another person until you have "walked a mile in their shoes."

The apostle Paul said, "But for the grace of God there go I."

## "Can't Buy Me Love"

Most of us assume that the wealthy are totally fulfilled. "They must be happy, they are rich!" we say to ourselves, trying to imagine what it would be like to be able to buy anything we desire.

Remember these words from an old Beatles' song, "Can't buy me love, love. Money can't buy me love?" If anybody has experienced the truth of that statement, it should be John, Paul, George, and Ringo.

The truth is, once all the material needs of a person have been filled, most people begin to look elsewhere for purpose and meaning in life. Everything in life becomes anticlimactic.

If people don't fill their lives with rewarding ways to meet their inner need for love, chaos will result. Eventually, the very assets they are striving to obtain will begin to choke them to death. This is why many rich and famous people are so unhappy and unfulfilled.

Could this be why wealthy Hollywood stars attach themselves to certain charities and spend hundreds of hours raising money for pet projects? Members of America's aristocracy seek to use their wealth and influence in political and humanitarian pursuits.

Even Princess Diana — at one time the most envied woman on earth — sought to drown her personal pain in acts of goodwill toward the poor and suffering. While many of her causes were noble and helpful, their main purpose was to satisfy an inner emptiness. I doubt that even Diana's hefty divorce settlement was ever able to buy her happiness; much less the love she so desperately longed for. We cannot imagine what it would be like to be part of the most powerful and famous royal family on earth, but we can relate to the fact that money and power has nothing to do with happiness.

## Marriage and Materialism

All my life I heard that "money doesn't buy happiness." I never truly understood the meaning behind that cliché until I became an investment advisor to many wealthy people and discovered the problems money causes.

The brilliant John Gray, Ph.D., author of *Men are from Mars, Women are from Venus,* writes in his chapter, "Women Are Like Waves," that money sometimes creates problems in a marriage. I could not agree more.

In counseling with married couples over the years, I have learned from observing people that financial disagreements can create very volatile situations.

One afternoon a few years ago, I was asked to meet with a seemingly well-to-do couple who was in financial trouble.

"My wife's spending habits are out of control," the husband told me, "and I can no longer afford to foot the bill for all the expensive things she buys."

"How is that affecting your marriage?" I asked.

"It is falling apart," the husband said bluntly.

The wife sat quietly listening, obviously embarrassed and distressed.

"To make matters worse," the man continued, "she was treasurer of a local organization and ..." he stopped for a moment. Then with his voice cracking from shame and bitterness, said, "She stole money from the group's funds to buy things she didn't even need."

All I could do was stare at the man in disbelief as I took in this shocking disclosure.

"Has that issue been resolved?" I finally asked.

"Yes," the husband told me. "A legal judgment was rendered, but now I am responsible for paying back all the money."

As part of my counseling, I was permitted to read a psychological report on the wife that revealed the source of her problem. Although on the surface they appeared to have a very happy, normal marriage, the husband in his quest to preserve capital had allowed his wife few luxuries even though they could afford a decent lifestyle.

When I mentioned this statement from the report, the wife finally broke her silence, "Yes," she told me. "I resented living far out in the country, driving up a dirt road, and residing in a house that needed fixing up."

Then sobbing into her hands, she blurted, "I lashed out by spending every dime I could get my hands on."

"Until the money ran out?" I asked gently.

"Yes," she mumbled with a deep sigh.

"Then you resorted to stealing," I stated.

She merely looked at me and nodded.

We tried to work out a financial solution to deal with the missing money, but that did not prevent the wife from being tried, convicted, and sentenced. Fortunately, she was placed on probation and required to perform community service with no incarceration.

I could only imagine the tremendous stress this placed on their already shaky marriage.

## Keeping Up With the Neighbors

Materialism can destroy a marriage. Another couple I counseled was on the verge of divorce because the wife kept the family in a constant state of panic trying to keep up with the neighbors.

"She is stealing money from me and spending it on the kids," the husband said angrily.

"What is she buying?" I asked candidly, not worrying about the wife's feelings as much as the obvious stress this habit was creating.

"She buys mainly clothes and tennis shoes," he said.

"Is this true?" I asked looking directly at the embarrassed spouse.

"Yes," she answered quietly.

"Why?"

"Because our neighbor's kids have more than our kids, and I don't want our kids to be embarrassed because they don't have as much," she answered.

I really wanted to grab this lady and shake her but that wouldn't be professional. What I did say had a profound effect on the wife and the husband.

"If you give your kids a choice of shoes that keeps them in pace with the neighborhood kids or give them the choice as to which one of you they want to live with, they would rather go barefooted."

That story had a happy ending. The kids grew up with less and kept their parents to raise and nurture them in the Lord.

## Planning and Dreaming

It seems to me that couples who are working together to achieve financial stability in their marriage — at any level of income — have the happiest and most fulfilling marriages. Why? Because they tend to lean on one another.

Unlike the rich, couples with few resources often plan and dream together, which results in sharing ideas and striving toward a common goal. This creates a bond of unity in which each spouse's emotional needs are met.

Middle and low-income couples often possess another advantage. They aren't distracted by cumbersome material possessions or expensive hobbies that take time away from the home and the marriage.

Conversely, being financially insecure can create negative feelings of disappointment. If the spouse complains all the time because she doesn't have enough and blames the husband for their destitute state, or vice versa, then life can be miserable. Soon the marriage falls apart because of the financial pressure. The material needs are not met by the party made responsible and trouble ensues.

Wives can put too much pressure on the husband to be the sole support of the family. In this day and age, it is nearly impossible for the family to exist on one income.

I certainly believe it is healthier for the wife to be at home with the kids. In some cases, however, more pressure results when couples try to eke out a living on one salary than is caused when both spouses work and cooperate to keep the family running smoothly.

I knew a couple who took a vow that only the husband would work outside the home. When circumstances prevented this man from retaining his job, no relief came from the wife because of the stringent ideal to which they were bound. The marriage blew apart when neither could adjust to the lifestyle of poverty.

I never thought I would ever say this, but, struggling is good for a marriage. Working out financial problems together as a couple strengthens the bonds between a husband and wife. Emotional needs are met as they both work to meet a common goal. When the struggle to make ends meet is over, the couple must have something else to fill their need for each other.

The struggle, however, should never be one-sided. Some men put all the responsibility on their wives. She pays the bills, does all the shopping, and runs the finances of the home. In other households, the opposite is true. The husband does not include the wife in the business affairs of the home, and he makes all the important decisions.

Whether there are one or two incomes, every home should be an equal economic arrangement. Marriage is a covenant relationship and should function that way. Emotional needs are met while sharing with each other and coming to agreements on how money should be spent. Every home should have a budget and pay strict attention to it.

Here are 10 ways to keep the financial area of your marriage in perspective and be satisfied that material things are not dominating your life.

1. **Have a joint checking account.**
2. **Balance the checking account together.**
3. **Set up a budget and stick to it.**
4. **Make joint spending decisions.**
5. **Give a little more than you take from the other.**
6. **Spend some money on each other occasionally.**
7. **Be willing to do whatever you can to solve a sudden unexpected financial crisis.**
8. **Never complain about your financial situation; talk it out.**
9. **Get professional financial counseling early into a problem.**
10. **Pay tithes from your income to your church.**

When circumstances change financially — either up or down — you will find out what your marriage is made of. If its entire foundation was built on material gain and the income level drops, the marriage will fall like a tree struck by lightning. However, if the marriage is built on the right foundation of love and understanding, then the partners will lock arms and begin over again.

Years ago, I met a Kentucky gentleman who held up three fingers and told me: "We started over three times! My wife and I never gave up."

In spite of financial hardships and disappointments, they remained happily married and worked together until they achieved financial success.

## Marriage and Money

I've dealt with many divorces. Through the ministry and as a professional financial advisor, 80 percent of the divorces I have dealt with have problems directly traced to a financial problem in the marriage.

I have just completed the DVD series, Financial Communication in the Marriage. In those videos, I deal with four basic problems that can cause a marriage to blow apart if they are not taken care of early on in the relationship. The videos deal with:

1. **Abdication of Responsibility**
2. **Spending Habits**
3. **Procrastination**
4. **Hasty Decision Making**

They also offer advice as to how to avoid these things or fix them.

By the time you are reading this book, you can enhance your knowledge and protection of your marriage by buying these DVDs. They come with a workbook so a couple can work through the series, enhance the marriage, and fix financial problems.

## The Financial Fallout

While discussing this chapter with one of my golfing buddies, he made an unusual confession right before tee off.

"I'm sticking with my wife because I can't afford a divorce," he said matter-of-factly.

Taken aback, I finally managed to reply, "That may not be the best reason for keeping up a marriage, but it certainly is one to be considered."

After that incident, I decided to include in this book a discussion of certain aspects that need to be considered when a divorce is possible. If people realize the financial consequences of divorce, they might be less likely to violate the marriage and instead try to avoid divorce at all costs. Perhaps we would not let our petty differences escalate into small-scale wars if we knew how deleterious the consequences would be in the end.

No matter who is at fault or who initiates the proceedings, divorce can wreck a household and plunder the material wealth of both husband and wife. After the former partners have dealt with all the emotional trauma of a divorce, the most calamitous and crushing feature remains — the financial chaos. Unless you are independently wealthy, you and your spouse could easily end up financially crippled for the rest of your lives.

While every situation has its own set of problems, one factor remains the same: divorce is expensive. In most divorce cases, both parties usually end up with attorneys' fees to pay, court costs, and other unexpected expenses.

When one party sues another for divorce, the costs can be heavy depending upon the difficulty of the case. Unfortunately, for the one being sued for divorce, he or she in most cases must pay his or her own expenses. Hiring an attorney is always expensive.

While some attorneys charge a flat fee for a divorce, family practice lawyers charge hourly rates, ranging from $300 an hour and more.

## Arbitrating a Settlement

If children are involved, the courts in various states look at divorce in favor of the mother. A judge or arbitrator will take several factors into consideration: whether the wife has been working outside the home; how much money she can earn; and the ability of the husband to support the children and the wife. These issues determine how much money and property the court will award to the spouse.

The matter of alimony and child support, however, is only part of the financial chaos a divorce can render.

In California, the court will often allow the settlement to take place without the parties appearing in court. This is permitted if both the husband and wife can settle their differences without the courts intervention. Lawyers draw up the settlement, both parties sign it, the judge approves it, and that is the end of it — unless the settlement is later violated or one of the parties wants a change for some reason.

A man I knew left his wife and four children, moved in with another woman, and announced his intention to divorce. The wife did not want to go to court and be dragged through the embarrassment of a public divorce settlement. Since I was very close to both the husband and wife, and both trusted me, I was asked to arbitrate the settlement.

The husband, thinking our friendship would work to his advantage and that this arrangement would be the cheapest for him, anticipated a settlement in his favor. Believing I would be fair, the husband and wife had previously agreed they would abide without question to the terms of the settlement I proposed.

When the three of us met with the attorney in his office to settle the dispute, I began by explaining my reasons for the settlement I was about to propose.

"When the wife has spent her life serving the husband and has given up what skills she could have acquired through life to raise children and keep the home," I explained, "she should not be required to get a full-time job and pay her own way."

Although I could sense the husband beginning to tense up, I didn't back down. Looking him square in the face, I said, "The husband still has the responsibility to support the wife, keeping the income as much in balance for the support of her and the kids as possible. When the children are raised, he should still keep supporting her until she decides to remarry. Even then, it is the father's responsibility to support the children until they are 18 years of age, even if the spouse marries again."

I knew I was on solid ground since my opinion concurs with that of the courts in California and other states. Most states will find in favor of the wife and mother but probably not as heavily as I settled this case. I have been to law school, so I knew how to settle this case based on the laws and experience.

As the husband wiped the perspiration from his forehead, I continued. "If a man decides to interrupt the lives of others who are dependent upon him, then he should have to pay," I said frankly.

The exception to this would be in cases where the wife is having an affair outside the home. If she chooses that route, custody of the kids should be given to the husband, and the wife left to her own volition.

Coming to an agreement between two parties involves many variables, and it may seem impossible to settle a divorce outside the rigors of a court case. But you can, and if you do, it will be less costly on both parties.

## Who Gets the House?

Lifetimes are spent accumulating wealth and precious possessions. The purchase of a home early in a marriage is an exciting time. Over the years the couple upgrades their house until finally, in mid-life, their home reaches the point where everything is exactly as they had planned.

Divorce enters the picture, and the unsettling effects of a marriage breakup begin to unwrap the couple's neatly packaged lifestyle. Piece-by-piece precious mementos, furniture, automobiles, and other personal items, become what the court calls "property."

When you divorce, all property that you and your spouse own is valued and lumped together. The total of your assets is then divided between the two of you. Depending on where you live, you may or may not receive equal shares.

"Community Property" states — which are Arizona, California, Idaho, Louisiana, Nevada, New Mexico, Texas, Washington, and Wisconsin — generally consider both spouses as equal owners of all their shared property. In other words, each spouse receives 50 percent of the real value of the property.

Other states do not consider spouses to be equal owners of the value of their marital property. These are called "Non-Community Property" states and use certain criteria like length of the marriage, whether each spouse worked outside the home, the spouse's job skills, etc., to determine how the property is divided.

Sometimes the home goes to one of the spouses. Most of the time, however, the home is put up for sale, and the proceeds are divided between the two divorcing parties. At that point, neither person has enough money to replace the quality of house — or the standard of living — they had previously enjoyed together.

Recently, two of my good friends divorced. Everything was divided equally, and whatever could be sold was sold. In the end, the couple was forced to live in separate rented apartments far below the standard of the beautiful home they had to sell.

Another friend told me, "I moved back in with my ex-wife because it was too expensive for us to live separately."

"Really?" I asked, shocked by this recent development.

"Yeah," he replied, "but nothing has changed. We have no intention of getting remarried."

Although, I do not morally condone this kind of economic solution, I understand the financial fallout divorce causes.

The old adage, "two can live cheaper than one," certainly applies when it comes to divorce. Two people sharing a house with double incomes is cheaper than maintaining separate housing. Insurance costs, utilities, upkeep, etc., all raise the financial costs for the divorced person who hopes to maintain his or her previous standard of living.

Few people consider the aftermath of the break-up of their marriage. Let me acquaint you with one of the harshest realities: hundreds of thousands of divorced men and women will never again own a home. Unless they marry into a situation where the new spouse already owns a home or the two are able to combine their resources to purchase a house, the American dream will be nothing more than a sad memory.

## Married With Children?

When Larry decided he no longer wanted to be married, he separated from his wife and moved to a nearby town. When they finally divorced, Sue, who had never worked outside the home, was forced to sell their lovely, two-story suburban house and move into a subsidized two-bedroom apartment with her teenage daughters.

Larry pays support for the girls, spends a lot of time with them, and even helps Sue out once in a while. Sue now works for minimum wage at a day care center, drives an old, unreliable car, and has been left hanging — both emotionally and financially — for years.

This scenario could be repeated over and over again only with different names and changes in minor details.

A high percentage of divorced women are forced onto the welfare roles and into government subsidized housing projects from which they never escape. Many must take minimum wage jobs and/or return to school for more education and job-skill training. Young children are usually carted off to day care centers to be raised by strangers while older children grow up without the love and guidance of a father.

Combined with the emotional trauma of divorce, the financial adjustments add insult to injury.

After a divorce, only one parent can be considered by law to be the "custodial parent." If it is the wife, she gets to claim an exemption for the child on her income tax — unless she has agreed otherwise. This is true in spite of the fact that the ex-husband must pay child support, and the child may even live with the father a portion of the year.

Married people have another advantage when it comes to paying income taxes. As a married couple filing a joint return, you pay much less tax than a single person — especially if you have children. A single person, earning a yearly income of $50,000 pays nearly $2,000 more in income tax per year than a married couple filing jointly and earning the same amount. These figures change as income tax laws change, of course, but you get the point.

Another friend of mine is separated from his wife and has been for many years.

"Why don't you get a divorce?" I once asked.

"We don't want to," my friend replied.

"Why, if you're not living together?"

"Because," he explained, "we would have to file separate income tax returns, and that would cost both of us a bundle each year in extra taxes."

I have never done a survey, but I'll wager there are more of these situations in the United States than the government wants to admit.

The tax laws punish some couples and keep them living in limbo, making it impossible for them and their children to lead normal lives. If a person decides that celibacy is the lifestyle they desire, then they should not be executed financially by having to pay higher taxes.

Married people have another advantage over those who are divorced or single. It is cheaper to be married and pay health insurance for two people. Since divorcees must each pay the higher premium for a single person, health insurance costs increase.

This is another reason why divorced mothers without adequate job skills are forced to depend upon the government. Without Medicaid assistance, their children would have no health insurance. If they earn over a certain amount of money, however, they lose the Medicaid. This forces them to stay in low-paying jobs and dooms them to a life of poverty.

## What's Yours is Mine!

As an investment advisor and firm owner, we did a lot of financial and estate planning, which means we often dealt with divorce settlements. One of the great illusions people have is concerning IRAs, such as 401k plans, 403b plans, and other retirement vehicles.

Many people planning for divorce do not realize that the other party has a right to those savings. In a divorce settlement, these cases are settled by the court when no voluntary forfeiture or agreement is made by the parties to split these assets.

A former client of mine divorced, but his spouse had no idea of certain IRAs he had socked away throughout the years. At the time the divorce settlement was agreed upon, he made no mention of the hidden assets. His opinion was they were his investments: he had earned them and had taken the initiative to save the money, so it really was none of his spouse's business at that juncture.

One day his ex-wife called me to discuss her situation. I was only a few days out of the business but since I maintain all the financial records on every client I have ever had for life, sensitive information is available.

"Could you check to see how the joint accounts my ex-husband and I owned settled? I need my part of the money to make a down payment on a new car," she explained.

I referred the problem to one of the firm's sales assistants. The sales assistant proceeded to mistakenly identify two separate IRAs the other party owned. This would normally be a breach of confidence even concerning a married partner who was not an authorized signature on the account. The sales assistant, however, assumed the IRAs would be part of the settlement since that is normal. The spouse did not know about the separate account.

The irate wife hired an attorney, forced me to release the assets, and then sued me for trying to collaborate with the husband to hide the assets. Although she lost my part of the case, it still cost me a couple thousand dollars to prove my innocence. The husband, however, had to divest himself of the assets he thought were clearly his.

In a situation like this, the IRAs and other investment vehicles by which assets are invested — and of which a portion rightfully belongs to the spouse — could be rolled over. In this particular case, the wife decided to cash in the IRAs, pay the penalty and taxes, and take the money left over. If she had decided not to take out the money, then the investments would have been rolled into an IRA for her, and the tax-deferred account would take its normal course as if it belonged to her all the time.

In some cases, only half of the money leaves investment accounts. In others, I have seen more than half an IRA go to the government in the form of taxes and penalties incurred by cashing in early in order to pay for the divorce. Few people realize how a divorce can jeopardize their retirement assets.

According to John Ventura, author of the book, *The Small Business Survival Kit,* small-business owners face another risk when it comes to divorce. He writes, "Depending on the laws of your state, once you are married, half or a portion of the future income your business generates, the property that income purchases, and the amount your business appreciates may be viewed as the property of both you and your spouse."

This is true even if the husband or wife has never worked for the business or helped out financially. All that matters is that you were married when the business was established.

On the other hand, "in all states," Mr. Ventura writes, "what you own prior to your marriage is yours alone, even after marriage."

You are probably beginning to realize why more and more couples are opting for pre-nuptial or post-nuptial agreements to protect their property and assets in case of a divorce.

If you are considering divorce — or if divorce seems inevitable — let me explain the cold, hard facts.

First of all, divorce is not only devastating to the individuals involved, but to the children — regardless of their ages — to grandchildren, to other close family members, and also to the friends who love and honor you. I used to think that putting off divorce until the kids were grown wasn't the best policy; I still believe it is very important for two people to settle their disputes after the children have left home if they can. The situation can become worse, however, if the disputes that remain unresolved become violent and daily threaten the children and their security.

No matter what the circumstances, children are always the unfortunate victims in any divorce. Every child wants his or her parents to remain together even if it means that the home life becomes difficult. No child wants his parents to break up unless violence or some other unstable condition exists that cannot be rectified.

If the children are age 18 or older, the trauma of a custody battle is avoided. Still, I have counseled with post-teens who were devastated emotionally by the break-up of their family.

Adult children, of course, have their own lives and families and can adjust much quicker, making the overall impact on them not as great. Older children, however, face a unique challenge: that of dealing with the emotions of each parent and walking a thin line between the two so as not to alienate one from the other. I know families who are still fragmented and estranged from other members because one child sided with a certain parent during the divorce proceedings.

Not only must adult children adjust to their parents being apart but also to the effect it will have on their own children. Years of happy family memories are replaced by the strain of the present. Holidays and special occasions are now tainted by an uncomfortable uncertainty that forces adult children to constantly choose. Should we invite Dad if Mom is coming for Thanksgiving dinner? What about Sue's graduation? Or Tom's wedding?

Like ripples in a pond caused by a tossed stone, the effects of divorce spread out to affect a wide spectrum of relationships. Mothers, fathers, brothers, sisters, brothers-in-law, sisters-in-law, nephews, nieces, grandparents, aunts, uncles, and cousins can all be emotionally attached to an ex-wife or husband.

My brother Val Mark once said, "She's been my sister-in-law for 29 years, and I love her."

Close friends are also affected. My best friend, upon learning that one of our mutual best friends had divorced, phoned me and said, "My whole family is devastated by this."

When one of my business associates told me he was thinking about divorce, I tried my best to talk him out of it. Our family loved his wife and children, and it was going to be hard to adjust after a lifelong friendship without the two of them being together.

## Clear Disadvantages

For anyone thinking about divorce, I hope after reading this chapter you will have second thoughts. Divorce is not always the answer to marital problems. Things can be worked out.

Marriage counselor Michele Werner Davis writes in her book, *Divorce Busting: A Revolutionary and Rapid Program for Staying Together,*

"Ultimately what dissolves the marriage are not differences but hopelessness. This usually happens when one of the partners thinks the future is just a miserable extension of the past."

Divorce causes a lot more pain than most people realize. When you have lived with someone for many years and then end a marriage because of difficulties left untended, you may end up unfulfilled and very empty inside.

Although divorce creates havoc in the lives of those directly affected by its devastating results, most divorcees eventually adjust. If life follows its normal course, relationships will be repaired, and much of the tension caused by divorce will reside as time passes. Of course, this is not true in every case. I have friends who will testify that after several years they still have not fully recovered; some never will.

The aftermath of a divorce depends on how devastating the divorced parties want it to be. If they remain bitter and vindictive, then reparation will not come easily. If they forgive as much as they can, then amends can be made between the two parties to keep from dividing their loved ones.

Some divorcees leave town to avoid the pain of constant memories or the embarrassment of being alone. When the ex spouses cannot exist in the same location, one or the other must often move away in an effort to achieve peace of mind. For some, this is a positive step. For others, the stress of leaving their roots behind and starting over in a strange place creates even greater loneliness.

"We've begun to realize that divorce has clear disadvantages," David writes. "It rarely solves the problem that it is intended to solve. Too many people get out of the marriage only to find similar problems in future marriages or single life."

I urge anyone considering divorce to seek counseling before throwing in the proverbial towel. You will both be much better off financially and emotionally if the marriage can be saved.

# CHAPTER SIX

# BANKRUPTCY: THE LAST RESORT

When you picked up this book and read the chapter titles, did you immediately turn to this chapter?

Many do. For several reasons.

I entered law school late in life. I was not interested in the practice of law for a living; I wanted to add to the knowledge I had, so I could become the best and most informative counselor I could possibly be. I wanted to be able to give expert advice as a means of answering those inevitable questions that had been coming to me for a long time. I was most interested in, and paid particular attention to, the laws concerning bankruptcy. Today, our economy is in shambles, and that education is paying off for those who seek my advice from a legal and Scriptural viewpoint.

Some people are searching for ways to avoid bankruptcy. Many are considering it and want information about bankruptcy and its financial ramifications. Others, like the millions every year who file for personal and business bankruptcy, are looking for emotional stability while going through it. Few issues create more fear and dread than the word "bankruptcy." It is amazing to me how many people know nothing about it, and the fear has driven many to suicide.

I counsel on a regular basis with people who want to work their ways out of financial stresses. Most of those people I can help, but there are a few I cannot. When I realize there is no hope, I begin to counsel them on the Scriptural attitude about bankruptcy and prepare them to handle it emotionally. Many times these people feel better just being able to talk to someone who can help them divulge their fears.

People on the verge of bankruptcy often ask me questions like these:

"Is filing for bankruptcy morally wrong?"

"What effect will the aftermath of bankruptcy have on my life?"

"What will my friends, neighbors, family, and business associates think of me?"

"How will financial failure affect my credit report?"

"Will I be able to repair that credit rating in the future?"

Let's deal with these very serious issues.

## Is it Right or Wrong?

Do I believe in bankruptcy? Yes and no.

I want to point out that some Christian organizations that give financial advice and try to help people function make a huge mistake by not recognizing when a person has trouble that cannot be fixed.

I received a call a short time ago from a lady I did not know.

"Dr. Smith," she began, "You don't know me, but my friend said you can help me. My name is Cara."

"Tell me your story," I replied.

"I am destitute. I have lost my job and haven't paid my mortgage payments for several months. Finally, the bank is going to foreclose on me. My husband left me and ran off to another state, and I have no one to help me."

"Have you had any financial counseling?" I asked.

"Yes. I have been attending a financial class at a church, but they have not been able to come up with answers."

"Have you considered bankruptcy?" I asked boldly.

"Oh, no, they told me that was wrong and God would punish me for doing something like that. I don't have enough faith."

When she told me that, I knew exactly what organization had been dealing with her. "Can you come to my house in an hour?"

"Yes I can, but aren't you busy?" she asked timidly.

"I'm always busy, but you need help right now," I insisted.

I listened to Cara's sordid details of a life that had begun with an inheritance, and a husband who wasted all the money on foolishness. I also learned she was abused which is how the rogue got the money from her in the first place. Cara was destitute and over-the-top financially. Nothing could help her except to get out from under the incessant phone calls that were stressing her to the max. Until her husband left, she had paid all her bills, but now could not afford the credit card debts and other bills he left her owing.

Cara was terrified of bankruptcy beyond the normal fears that people have when contemplating the alternative. She had bought into the interpretation that bankruptcy was wrong and sinful, and that she lacked faith in God.

In less than 20 minutes, I changed Cara's mind. I explained that the philosophy of bankruptcy being non Biblical is an ignorance of God's Word; it was God who came up with the plan to begin with. We get our laws concerning lending and borrowing from the Old Testament Law. Bankruptcy, as I will explain later in this chapter, was part of those laws. I helped her understand she was not dirty and vile because she would have to forfeit her already ruined credit and seek help in a court of law.

"You have saved my life," she said over and over as the burdens were lifted from her soul.

Bankruptcy is hard enough on an individual without the prolonged problem of being harassed to death by creditors.

The bankruptcy laws exist for a good purpose. Preventing unrelenting creditors from completely devastating a person for the rest of his life has Scriptural basis. As far back as Old Testament times people had trouble paying their debts and were hounded by their creditors. The bankruptcy laws are based on Biblical principles and relate back to the time when the Israelites were given the laws of God.

## Let's Take a Brief Look at Those Bible-Based Laws

### 1. Bankruptcy laws are based on forgiveness and mercy.

The fathers of our country understood that the Bible taught the forgiveness of debt under some extreme circumstances. People who get in financial trouble and have no way out can go to the courts and get relief. This law of our land comes from the **Book of Deuteronomy 15:1,2.** *"At the end of every seven years that shalt make a release. And this is the manner of the release: Every creditor that lendeth aught unto his neighbor shall release it; he shall not exact it of his neighbor, or of his brother; because it is called the Lord's release (KJV)."*

Seven years is significant because our bankrupt laws prohibit a debtor from seeking release from that debt only once every seven years. This is significant because that is enough time for a person to get back on his feet and does not permit the abuse of the law by those who are dysfunctional and want to use the system to gain.

### 2. Under Bible bankruptcy laws, the debtor gets to keep certain assets that allow him to re-establish himself.

Debt was considered bondage in the Old Testament. Therefore, the following verses show the attitude toward the bondage of servants who were obligated to their duty and then released under the law.

*"And if thy brother, and Hebrew man, or a Hebrew woman, be sold unto thee, and serve thee six years; then in the seventh year thou shalt let him go free from thee. And when thou sendest him out free from thee, thou shalt not let him go away empty: Thou shalt furnish him liberally out of thy flock, and out of thy floor, and out of thy winepress: of that wherewith the Lord thy God hath blessed thee thou shalt give unto him. And thou shalt remember that thou wast a bondman in the land of Egypt, and the Lord thy God redeemed thee: therefore I command thee this thing today." Deuteronomy 15:12-15 (KJV).*

It is not enough to complain that debtors should not be released from their obligations after they have been stripped of their non-exempt assets because "the debtor is obligated to pay his bills." God could say the same thing to the unbeliever that it is too bad for the sin; He condemns us anyway. Under that thinking, no one would ever go to heaven without the mercies of God.

### 3. Jesus said to forgive our debtors.

Debt is sin in the Lord's Prayer. "Forgive those who sin against us." Monetary debts that cannot be paid fall into the category of a sin that needs forgiveness.

Sin creates a Spiritual debt that cannot be paid except by death. Mercy declares that debt paid for on the Cross.

Likewise, justice says you are to pay your debts and that is the right and Scriptural thing to do. There are also wages attached to not paying debts. However, mercies of the law allow you to obtain forgiveness of your obligations if you cannot pay them back.

What was Jesus' attitude toward debtors that couldn't pay?

Matthew 18:23-35 tells the parable of the servant who begged for forgiveness, and the Lord had compassion on him and forgave his debts. It is also the illustration of what happens when you have obtained mercy but refuse to give mercy to someone else. Shakespeare said in a paraphrase of this verse: "What man seeketh mercy rendering none."

*"And when they had nothing with which to repay, he freely forgave them both." Luke 7:42 (KJV)*

Jesus gave us a "new beginning" by forgiving our sins. Our country is willing to forgive debts and give those people needing mercy a "new beginning."

Arguments can be made forever, and I can write a book on this one subject. Some bankrupt laws may seem unfair, and many attorneys disagree with the new laws that require a re-organization (Chapter 13) before a straight bankruptcy (Chapter 7) can be filed.

Our bankruptcy laws are fair. You cannot bankrupt from taxes, cash infusions derived from fraud, restitution, fines, and other crimes of deliberate wrong doing that have a monetary penalty. This keeps the laws in check and the crooks in better balance.

The purpose of this law in our country is to permit the debtor from being so discouraged that they are tempted to fling into uncontrollable debt again. It gives them something to establish after the financial failure.

I believe bankruptcy should occur only under extenuating circumstances where it cannot be avoided. Let me explain.

Suppose someone has a huge hospital bill because of a prolonged illness, and their health insurance will not cover all the costs; that person could be wiped out financially if there were no other means of assistance such as state and local agencies or charitable interests to help. Hospitals are brutal at collecting debts and will take all the steps necessary by law —and that is their right.

On the other hand, in certain cases the bankruptcy laws are too lenient. Sometimes it is too easy for people to march into bankruptcy court and abdicate their debts with little recourse for the creditors. The ease with which the court discharges people from their financial obligations has made bankruptcy very popular.

The misinformation surrounding bankruptcy serves to complicate the problem. Some people are misled by their attorneys who advise bankruptcy in order for their clients to re-establish their credit rating. Nothing could be further from the truth.

After filing for bankruptcy and being discharged by the court from their debts, many people discovered that re-establishing credit was next to impossible.

## Too Late?

A few years ago, I was lecturing at a large church in the Washington D.C. area. Afterwards, a lady — let's call her Mrs. Miller — came up and asked if she could talk with me privately.

During our discussion, I discovered Mrs. Miller and her husband were considering bankruptcy. It seems they had started a business out of their home in order to make more money. Having barely any capital and little experience, they entered into a great deal of debt in order to stock inventory. As the weeks wore on, the business floundered, debts mounted, and they found themselves with their backs against the wall, unable to pay their creditors. I couldn't help but wonder why Mrs. Miller's husband had not come along to talk with me. In fact, I never spoke with the man at all.

Over the years, I have found this to be a common occurrence when financial disaster looms imminent. One of the spouses abdicates the responsibility and leaves the other to do the worrying — as well as deal with the pressure of finding a solution.

This is one reason why I believe that 80 percent of all break-ups in marriage can be traced to some kind of financial ailment. It is a mistake for both the husband and wife not to share financial responsibility equally. When that doesn't happen, one partner always gets the blame, and the marriage suffers irreparable damage.

I found this to be the case with Mrs. Miller.

Not only was there a tremendous strain in the marriage, the stress on the wife was nearly unbearable. Mrs. Miller was strapped with finding an answer to their financial troubles.

That particular night the threat, dread, and fear of bankruptcy forced her to reach out for answers.

"The thought of entering bankruptcy court and dismissing our obligations is more than I can bear," Mrs. Miller told me, her voice shaking.

"I know you do not want to live with the reputation of not paying your bills," I said reassuringly. "I suggest you write down everything you can think of concerning your financial situation and send it to me for study. I will see if I can come up with some answers to your problems."

The relief on her face was immediately apparent.

"Perhaps there is some gleam of hope I can find in the situation," I said with an encouraging smile.

Many times it is hard to share financial troubles with someone else. Admitting failure can be painful and embarrassing. Acknowledging the problem to someone else and seeking help, however, usually acts as a great stress reliever. Admitting you have a problem is the first step away from denial. Confessing to someone you view as important is a great stress reliever.

After receiving the requested papers in the mail, I reviewed the entire situation and then made the phone call I dreaded.

"I'm sorry, Mrs. Miller, there is nothing I can do," I said, noting that their credit was shot, credit cards repossessed, bank loans called, house foreclosed upon, cars repossessed, judgments and liens by creditors, and the bank account seized by the IRS. "It's too late."

She had waited too long to seek help.

My advice was earth-shattering to her, and one that I give very sparingly. In this case, there was no way out. She needed protection from the court.

"Bankruptcy is the only answer," I told her.

# Facing the Facts

While talking with a lady one day, she told me that she had filed for divorce.

"I'm sorry to hear that you and your husband could not make the marriage work after so many years together," I said sadly. "It must have been very difficult for you emotionally to face the reality that it was over."

I'll never forget what she told me next.

"Divorce is awful," she said. "But after months of anguish, the stress came mainly from my unwillingness to face the problem. Actually, the day I filed for divorce, I felt a hundred percent better."

Financial difficulties have the same result.

Anyone facing financial collapse must go through three emotional stages:

**1. Facing the reality of financial failure.**

**2. Deciding to file for bankruptcy.**

**3. Dealing with the consequences after the fact.**

Any major decisions we make in life that change our behavior, interrupt our habits, or alter our environment and upset us create stress.

Over the years, I have counseled many people who were going through the trauma of financial distress. The emotions involved have about the same degree of intensity as a marriage breakup, a death, a threatening health problem, or the loss of a job. In fact, all these problems could lead to financial failure and even more stress.

Losing everything you own can be devastating. At that point, the desperate person needs emotional help.

On many occasions, I have sat in my office across from counselees who are voicing all the fears racing around in their minds. On the verge of absolute despair, they will often repeat, "I don't know what I'm going to do. I don't know what I'm going to do."

After helping them realize that bankruptcy is the only choice, I have seen men and women cry with the same grief as if they had lost a child. Of course, I don't believe financial failure is on the same scale as the loss of a child, but the emotional trauma at the time can be almost as devastating.

How can a person face the reality of bankruptcy without having a nervous breakdown?

This is what I suggest: First, face the facts realistically. After you have tried everything you can to avoid bankruptcy, and you realize there is nothing else you can do, come to grips with the reality of the situation. This will help you deal with the problem.

## Deciding to File

A few months after I told Mrs. Miller that bankruptcy was her only way out, I got another call — one I will never forget.

Mrs. Miller was in her pastor's office, and he suggested they phone me.

"I can't face the embarrassment of bankruptcy," she sobbed. "I would rather die!"

Since I was the one who initially suggested this (her attorney and others later advised the same), she thought I should share in her emotional plight, which she indicated might end in suicide.

"Please, please, help me find another answer. I can't stand it any longer. Bill collectors are calling every day, and my creditors are constantly after me to pay them. Please help me!" she pleaded almost uncontrollably.

There was nothing else I could do. I found myself at a loss for words.

"Oh cheer up. Everything will work out," just didn't seem right at that moment.

I then began to search my own conscience and came up with some advice that I have used time and again for similar situations.

"Let me make a suggestion," I said slowly. "You have the option of not filing bankruptcy, but this would not relieve the pressure generated by your creditors' relentless pursuit of the money you owe them."

I was careful not to continue to push for bankruptcy. I clearly understood that this lady was on the verge of suicide; in fact, her pastor told me that before Mrs. Miller and I began this conversation.

I also realized that if she didn't seek help from the court, she could never recover and would possibly lose her sanity or her life through health problems or some other disaster. There is no material possession worth that risk.

"I think you should go to your attorney and start the proceedings," I suggested.

It was what I inserted into her mind next, however, that made all the difference in how things were going to turn out.

I said, "Go to the attorney and file bankruptcy, but do it with this idea in mind. The court will protect you from the creditors so you can get back on your feet. But you should never think you don't still owe the debt. Just because you take bankruptcy doesn't mean you are debt or scot-free."

"What do you mean?" she interrupted between sobs.

"Go into the court with the idea that not only do you still owe the money, but that with God's help you intend with all your might to pay it back," I explained. "In other words, if you ever do get straightened out so that you have an infusion of cash, pay the money back to the creditors."

Using this approach, an honest person can remain honest. This is why the bankruptcy laws are part of our judicial system. They come from the Bible. In fact, almost every culture on earth has or has had a system of relieving a person with insurmountable debt from the threat of relentless creditors, and it is against the law in the United States to incarcerate or put a person to death for debt. We didn't arrive at the laws for frivolous reasons.

"I believe that you and your husband are honest people," I assured her. "You have made honest mistakes and are now paying for them."

Almost immediately she stopped sobbing. "Oh, thank you so much," she said with relief telling in her voice. "I had not considered that approach. I really appreciate your taking the time to advise me."

Facing the facts is the best therapy to attack any negative situation. The main cause of stress caused by bankruptcy results from feeling guilty and tainted. If you bury that emotion and look at the problem as a business decision, it is much easier to handle.

I heard Robert Schuller say once, "Pray with zest, face the test, do your best, forget the rest."

## Making Up Your Mind

Once you have made up your mind to file for bankruptcy, you should follow these basic steps:

**1. Be informed.**

Read all you can about the different kinds of bankruptcy and which one relates to your situation. The "Bankruptcy: Questions and Answers" Appendix at the end of this book provides information about the legal issues involved.

Many people who file for bankruptcy are not aware of the issues or ramifications beforehand. Knowledge always puts you in greater control.

Don't allow yourself to become a victim of your circumstances.

**2. Find a good attorney.**

Some people fall prey to a greedy bankruptcy lawyer who makes his living advising people to abdicate their debts in court while he rakes in what's left of their hard-earned money.

"If you want to get out of trouble fast," the usual pitch goes, "file for bankruptcy then no one can touch you."

Instead of sound advice, these desperate people get put on the fast track to bankruptcy court by a smooth-talking lawyer who fails to give them all the facts.

Bankruptcy proceedings are expensive, but some attorneys charge much more than others. If your bankruptcy transactions are not complicated, the costs should be reasonable. The more complicated your case, the more expensive. Expect to pay most of the lawyer's fee up front.

Your attorney will guide you through all the steps that will take place. Talking to a concerned lawyer can be good therapy since it gives you an opportunity to share all your bottled-up tension.

Many people have told me that after talking to an attorney, they felt much better. Sometimes the lawyer can determine that you do not need to file for bankruptcy at all but will recommend that you meet with a professional financial advisor.

Recently, I have been working with several business people in their mid-30s to mid-40s helping them position themselves to make it through this current recession. They are too young to have gone through the last deep recession of 1979–1982. One of the attorneys in our church recommended a Christian attorney who does bankruptcy cases. My feelings were that we should look into Chapter 11 first before a straight Chapter 7. The attorney insisted that I come to the meeting with this lady because I was familiar with their entire operation after months of counsel.

"I'm sorry," the attorney said, "but Chapter 11 bankruptcy is very expensive, and you are beyond that. I would not even spend the money to file for Chapter 7 because that will do no good. I suggest you do a voluntary Chapter 7 and liquidate this business yourself."

Now that's an honest attorney, and he did not charge for the consultation.

**3. Stay on top of everything during the proceedings.**

Cooperate fully. Get your papers ready in a timely manner. When your attorney asks for something, don't procrastinate.

The quicker you get the deal over with, the sooner you can get on your feet and the easier you will be able to handle the accompanying emotions.

**4. If you cannot afford an attorney, sometimes a good independent paralegal can handle the proceedings and help you through it.**

In this city, I have a couple of paralegals who have done bankruptcies for my clients and have done an excellent and cost-effective job.

**5. Contact Legal Aid in your city.**

If you live in a town that is large enough, you probably have legal aid. There are knowledgeable people working there who will file a Chapter 7 for you. One of my clients recently filed for Chapter 7 and got through the proceedings for less than $500. Not a bad deal when an attorney cannot be afforded.

## Going to Court

There is no way to make filing for bankruptcy and going to court into a pleasant experience. This is why I recommend you get all the counseling and professional advice you can afford before you do it.

Having to admit failure creates tremendous emotional pressure.

Add to that a lack of understanding about bankruptcy and the fear of the unknown, and a person can become a basket case.

I have counseled people who came to my office wringing their hands in fear.

"Don't worry," I tell them. "We'll get you through this."

"But won't I have to go to jail?" they ask.

"No," I reassure them. "In the United States, it is unlawful for anyone to go to jail for debt. That's why the bankruptcy laws exist."

That bit of good news has changed many a countenance from pale horror to jubilation.

Aside from the legal issues, you need to consider the personal and emotional problems that result from the stress of the bankruptcy court.

You and your spouse — and any partners who are involved — must appear in court. All of you will then be required to face your creditors during the proceedings.

The bankruptcy judge will then ask, "Does anyone have anything to say about the procedure or have a question to ask?"

If your creditors are there, and one or two of them is hostile, the situation can get ugly.

When one of my clients and his wife filed bankruptcy, they entered the courtroom rather sheepishly and sat in the back. As they looked around the room, they were shocked to see many of their creditors.

"I had no idea they would be there," he told me later as he shared the pain and embarrassment of the situation. "My wife and I were asked to come to the front of the courtroom, take a seat, and face the crowd including the creditors that were present. When the judge asked if anyone had a question or wanted to make a comment, one of our creditors rose to his feet and shouted obscenities at us. He was immediately removed, but it was very humiliating."

Fortunately, the judge recommended my client and his wife be discharged from their debt. After court was dismissed, some of their creditors were waiting for them to come down the steps and publicly chastised them.

Talk about an unpleasant experience!

# Truth and Consequences

Some people are led to believe that if they file for bankruptcy, they will immediately be able to borrow all the money they need the next day, and their credit will be perfect.

Nothing could be further from the truth. Bankruptcy brings with it some dire consequences:

**1. You must be ready to give up your good reputation.**

You will now be known in the community for not paying your obligations. As a result, hardly anyone will give you credit for anything.

**2. Bankruptcies stay on your credit report for 10 years.**

Many people believe that seven years after a bankruptcy that their credit report is wiped clean. They get this confused with the right to file for bankruptcy the second or third time. You must wait seven years after filing for bankruptcy the first time before you can file again. Your credit report will reflect a bankruptcy for 10 years, and that is a long time to be without credit.

**3. You will not be able to get a credit card with a sizeable balance.**

During the 10-year period, no bank will issue a credit card to someone who took bankruptcy. The only bank card you can get is a secured card in which you put up a deposit as collateral against your balance. Eventually, credit card companies that charge high rates of interest will contact you, and you will have to put down a hundred or so dollars, pay a high rate of interest, monthly maintenance fees, etc., in order to have a $250 balance. However, if paid on time, creditors will gradually increase the credit limits that may or may not help your credit repair. Many credit applications ask if you have ever filed for bankruptcy. If you have, then you'll have to say so unless you want to falsify a credit application.

**4. You may not be able to buy a new car or a house.**

You could not even purchase a used car without a huge down payment or through a "buy here-pay here" transaction, which is very expensive. It will also be next to impossible for you to get a mortgage from a lending institution to buy a home.

Many people do not understand these severe consequences, and if they did, they would take more time considering alternative ways to pay their creditors. The person who moves on financially in spite of bankruptcy is the exception to the rule.

## Life After Bankruptcy

Throughout the process, keep in mind there is life after bankruptcy. In some cases, you can rebuild your financial life.

When I lived in Kentucky, a friend of mine had to declare bankruptcy. A wealthy man at one time, Bill was reduced to borrowing money from my partner and me for groceries.

My friend's experience, however, taught me a very valuable lesson and one that I have drawn from on numerous occasions.

After Bill and his wife recovered from the pain and embarrassment of having lost not only their livelihood but also the family business, they went into high gear.

Bill told me, "I don't need credit. I only need cash."

He was right.

Many people panic at their loss of credit after bankruptcy. Americans have become so accustomed to living with credit that we think we cannot live without it.

Bill was determined not to let the situation destroy him. Using creative thinking, he bartered his services and rebuilt the business without one dime from the bank or anyone else. He toughed it out.

In a few years, Bill had made enough money to restore everything he had lost, and he didn't owe anyone a penny. In fact, now he enjoys the privilege of having the banks seek him out as a depositor — and a borrower.

## Debtors and Creditors

Keep in mind that when you ask someone for credit, both of you take a risk. The debtor says he can pay the debt back and if he is responsible, he will do so. If extenuating circumstances derail his plans, however, he may have to seek protection from his creditors.

The creditor is saying he trusts this person to pay off the debt, but he takes the risk that something might happen to prevent the debtor from paying the debt in full. To offset that risk, he charges the debtor interest. Therefore the creditors shouldn't be crying for the heads of their customers and making their lives miserable if something legitimately goes wrong. If you take the risk and lose, deal with it.

Shortly after I finished college, a partner and I started a business supplying material to building contractors. Receivables were a necessary part of the operation, and we trusted our customers to pay us between the first and the tenth of the month. This is what the customer agreed to do when the goods were shipped. Sometimes, however, the customers were late paying their bills.

That winter was particularly harsh, and our customers were prevented from finishing the buildings they had started. Since the contractors had not completed their jobs, our customers could not pay their bills. This created downward pressure on us because we couldn't pay our suppliers. Our suppliers refused to wait until the spring thaw to get paid and forced us to shut down our business in order to get their money. What else could we do?

When we started our business, my partner and I were well aware of the risks involved in being undercapitalized. In addition, we gambled on the weather. We also knew we had to extend credit to the contractors in order to make it in the market. That was another risk we were willing to take.

A few months later, the weather cleared, our debtors paid their bills, and we paid ours. By then, it was too late. We were out of business and left without the start-up capital needed to jump back in.

It was at that point I decided I needed more education in order to operate in such a competitive marketplace with so many variables. Since then, I have made it all the way to a Ph.D. in Business Management and ended up in a different field altogether, but with the correct knowledge and attitude to maintain a business.

## Getting On With Your Life

As a person who has been in the financial pressure cooker more than once, allow me to make a few suggestions that will help you get back on your feet and on with your life:

### 1. Get counseling.

Don't try to go it alone. You may not be able to afford a professional counselor, but I suggest you seek out someone who can help you deal with the emotional repercussions of bankruptcy. Share with a friend or talk to your minister.

When you are under pressure, talking openly about your concerns and fears with others will provide a way to let off steam like the valve on an old-fashioned pressure cooker. The stress and tension must go somewhere.

## 2. Face the music.

Make no mistake about it. Some people will judge you harshly for filing bankruptcy.

I heard a preacher remark that bankruptcy was the ultimate slippage into the depths of mire. He said, "People who take bankruptcy are the worse of the worst."

That is ignorant foolishness. Swindlers won't be found in bankruptcy court because crooks always have another trick up their sleeves.

Financially busted people end up in court because something has gone wrong in their lives; it may be an unforeseen circumstance or a bad business decision. Sometimes it's the economy. Whatever the case, bankrupt people need help — which is what this book is about.

Family members will probably be the most critical because your actions reflect on them as well: but don't run away, that will only make matters worse. Eventually you will have to face your friends and family.

I have known people who moved away from their hometown after a financial failure only to make their situation worse. During hard times, you need your loved ones and familiar surroundings more than ever.

I would encourage someone to move to a different locale only if they can definitely better themselves. If the bankruptcy is caused by the loss of a job, then moving may be necessary. Keep in mind, however, that pulling up stakes is a stressful experience in and of itself at any time.

Don't try to hide the facts of your bankruptcy. You will be better off if you go about your business without considering whether anyone likes your decision or not. At this point, there is nothing you can do about it. Get on with life the very best way you can.

## 3. Make restitution, if possible.

Remember Mrs. Miller whom I mentioned earlier? For three years I had not heard a word from her and, in fact, had forgotten the incident altogether.

A few months ago, I was in the same location giving another lecture. Afterward, a lady walked up to me and said, "Dr. Smith, I will be forever grateful to you. You saved my life."

"How's that?" I asked in bewilderment, studying the glowing face before me.

"You remember. I am the one who was going to commit suicide rather than take bankruptcy, and your pastor friend called you for advice."

"Yes! Mrs. Miller!" I exclaimed. "What happened?"

"Last month I paid off the last debt I owed in bankruptcy with interest. And all my creditors are satisfied and shocked!"

As we talked, she told me how she was now getting on with her life. She also added that some of the creditors wouldn't even take the money because they had written off the debt. All of them said they would give her credit anytime she needed it, and her credit was stronger than ever.

Stop feeling guilty if you have filed for bankruptcy. Start living by promising yourself that someday, some way, you will take responsibility and catch up on some past mistakes. I promise you will be a better person for it.

### 4. Become financially responsible.

At times, I have recommended bankruptcy to my clients. I have done so however, only after studying their financial problems thoroughly and determining there was no other way out.

I then encourage the person to seek in-depth counseling about their money mismanagement and read as many books as they can in order to get a grip on their financial affairs.

Some people cannot handle credit of any kind. The only redeeming value of bankruptcy is that it forces those with out-of-control spending habits to operate without credit of any kind. Bankruptcy often makes them more responsible and appreciative.

If you are going to avoid bankruptcy, educating yourself in financial matters is the answer. Take some business classes at the local college or buy some money management books and learn how to function financially. Disciplining yourself to education and control could avoid desperate circumstances in the future.

## How to Avoid Personal Bankruptcy

When I lecture, I often end with a question and answer session.

Inevitably someone will ask, "Can you give us a list of suggestions on how to avoid financial trouble?"

Out of all the articles I have written on the subject, the following is my favorite quick-list checkup to functioning financially. If you can apply these simple steps before it's too late, you should be able to avoid financial crisis.

This list is not entirely original with me but includes a cross section of the opinions of most financial advisors. A more involved discussion of this list called "Seven Mistakes That Lead to Financial Chaos" appears in my book, *Exploding the Doomsday Money Myths.*

**1. Live within your means.**

Getting in over your head in debt or not balancing your spending against your income is the recipe for disaster. Learn to control where your money is going.

**2. Don't buy on impulse.**

Most of us are too quick to spend money.

How can you avoid impulse buying? Wait 24 hours before you make any sizable purchase. You will be surprised how much less appealing an item looks the next day after a good night's sleep.

**3. Avoid going into debt.**

The misuse of credit cards creates a tremendous financial burden. The millions of Americans who pay 15 to 22 percent in interest charges are being eaten alive by credit card debt.

Avoiding debt is the best policy, but if you need to take on some debt, do so for only a short time. This would exclude a home mortgage or investment property.

Do not try to get out of debt quickly. Manage your debt, or your debt will manage you.

Here are some suggestions for managing your debts (reprinted from *Exploding the Doomsday Money Myths, Why It's Not Time to Panic*):

1. Develop a plan for paying your debts. Write a list of your creditors, the amount of payment due, and the interest you are paying. Check to see if the interest you are paying exceeds the net rate of return of interest you are earning on your investments.

2. Pay off all negative interest loans from your savings accounts or liquid investments if they are not in IRAs or some sort of qualified tax-deferred plan.

3. Keep your short-term debt (everything except your mortgage) within a 36-month payback period.

   If you are making payments at a high rate of interest, get a loan at a lower rate of interest and pay off the debt, using a home equity loan is a good way of doing this. Invest the difference you were paying in a savings or investment account.

4. Use credit lines only in cases of emergencies. If you cannot control credit, don't use it.

5. Set up a budget. I have never come across a home, school, church, business or corporation in financial trouble that follows a budget. (I have made this point before, but I want to drive it home.) Many people feel that budgets are too confining and prevent them from spending. Quite the contrary, budgets allow you to spend the money you have.

6. Don't plunge into risky ventures without proper investigation. Remember the adage: If it sounds too good to be true, it probably is.

7. Save money. Most Americans could not survive financially for three to six months if they had an emergency. Why? Because they have no savings. Most households live from paycheck to paycheck.

   During a lecture I suggested that everyone needed to have savings amounting to three to six month's income. Afterwards, a man told me, "I couldn't live three to six days without a paycheck."

   Save 10 percent of your income and make it part of your budget. If you can't save that much, at least save something out of your check each week.

8. Prepare for the future. How? Here are some suggestions:
   a. Invest wisely by finding a professional financial advisor and see that he diversifies your investment portfolio.
   b. Refinance your home when interest rates are low enough. Invest the difference between the payment you are used to making and the new payment.
   c. Get disability insurance to protect yourself in case you become incapacitated and cannot earn an income.
   d. Raise your liability insurance higher than the worth of your home to protect your most valuable possessions.
   e. Make out a will. Don't put your family's future in jeopardy by leaving debts that must be settled and putting an undue burden on your family. If you have enough assets, you should check to see if you need a living trust. Registered financial advisors can help you with this.

If you follow these suggestions and others in this book, bankruptcy — barring some unforeseen financial disaster — will never be part of your future.

# CHAPTER SEVEN

# RETIREMENT AND BEYOND

As the dissertation topic for my Ph.D. in Business Management, I chose *"How Doomsayer Literature Creates Paranoia Among Conservative Christians."*

After preparing and administrating a national survey, I learned that many people are scared to death. In fact, I discovered that paranoia is not only very real, it's also widespread. At that point, I wished I had expanded the title to include all Americans, but the Christian side of the proposed model influenced the board of my secular university to approve the topic.

The "green" people are afraid pollution will destroy the earth's environment, the rain forests will disappear, and the sun will get so hot that the ice caps will melt. This will cause the ocean levels to rise and drown us all, or depending on whom

**America's paranoia goes beyond the economy.**

you believe, the sun will be obscured by industrial and automobile pollution, the temperatures will fall, and we will all freeze to death.

Some people are paranoid about the population boom. Fearing

that food shortages will lead to mass starvation, they advocate forced abortions and limiting the size of families. Others are afraid the sun will suddenly click off and throw the earth into a deep sleep killing everything on the planet.

During the Cold War, paranoia over a nuclear holocaust consumed many Americans. And with good reason since Soviet leader Nikita Khrushchev had pounded his shoe on the United Nations podium and shouted, "We will bury you!"

Back then it was the Russians who were going to get us; now we are afraid the Japanese and Chinese will bury us with their imports, or the Arabs will choke us to death on oil prices.

A recent PBS television program focused on how a giant asteroid could hit our planet at any time and destroy an entire civilization. The simulated devastation was awesome.

These are all future fears. What about present dangers?

I live in an earthquake zone where I survived the Bay Area quake of 1989. Believe me, nothing strikes more fear in the heart than having the ground shake and rumble beneath your feet. Some Californians have fled the state, fearing if their homes and lives aren't destroyed by an earthquake then surely a brush fire or a mud slide will do them in. While folks in other parts of the nation wonder why we don't all move east before California falls into the ocean, I can't help but consider the sanity of others — like those who build homes along the Atlantic coast where hurricanes keep pummeling the daylights out of them.

If we want to find something to be paranoid about, we can find it.

## Paranoia and Paradoxes

Nothing makes people more paranoid than the fear of losing all their money. Why does this fear produce such widespread anxiety among our population? Because the media takes great pleasure in reporting every doomsday prediction of financial collapse that comes down the pike. Book after book has been written in the past few years predicting our demise as a nation and threatening our soft lifestyles with a sudden hard landing.

The most difficult part of my job as a financial pastor, aside from giving free investment advice about money and planning for the future, is convincing folks not to worry constantly about their investments to the point of distraction — theirs and mine.

I realize that many issues both economic and social — are affecting our nation and creating concern and uncertainty about America's future. The purpose of this book, however, is not to address the fears associated with the environment, government spending, or nuclear warfare. My goal is to help you deal with the paranoia that affects you most: your financial condition — and the stress and pressure caused by that fear.

In dealing with people of all income levels, I have discovered an amazing paradox. Those who have no money are under pressure to make ends meet. Those who have money are under pressure to keep the ends from getting too close together.

Within both groups, two questions condense their fears:

1. **How can I keep from losing my present income so I can pay all the bills?**

2. **How can I preserve the money I have for a safe and comfortable retirement?**

Most people I deal with fall into the second category. They are worried about not having enough money for retirement. And those who worry the most are doing the least to ensure their retirement. Why? Because of fear.

Most of their fears are based on two common myths:

1. **Another Great Depression is imminent.**

2. **The Social Security System is going broke.**

In this chapter we will look at this second issue, examine it realistically, and see if there is any cause for great alarm. We will deal with the first fear in a later chapter.

## Is Social Security Going Broke?

As a frequent guest on television and radio talk shows around the country, I am consistently asked this question: "What is going to happen to our Social Security system?"

A two-hour program on an Orlando, Florida, radio station with Christian financial advisor Vinnie was designed to create controversy and allow callers to vent their rage over certain issues. As the guest that day, I took calls from irate senior citizens of the Sunshine State concerned about their future.

Many asked, "Will our Social Security system go broke and leave us without the retirement we have all been promised and have paid into all our lives?"

*Young and old alike are concerned about the future of Social Security.*

Worrying about the condition of Social Security is a full time job for many people; especially those who depend on it to supplement or completely support their retirement income. I worry about it too. Since I am paying the maximum Social Security tax allowable, I want to know if all the hard-earned money I have paid into it will be available to me.

Some folks are downright mad because they believe all the media hype about the Social Security System going broke.

Let's put aside all the hysteria and deal with the genuine question about what may or may not happen to Social Security. If we look at the facts, we can come to some logical conclusions.

## A Money-Sucking Monster?

After the Great Depression, many of the elderly were wiped out financially with no means of support, leaving them completely destitute.

The Social Security System, initiated in 1935 by President Franklin D. Roosevelt's Administration, was established to provide some form of income for citizens, who upon retirement, had no means of supporting themselves. President Roosevelt knew most people would not invest and would not save for their future needs.

The same is true today for many people; they could not survive financially without their monthly Social Security check. Although I hate paying the Social Security tax, which is mandatory, I still support the idea of giving our citizens a way of putting money aside for their golden years.

President Roosevelt knew the dangers of creating a system that would grow into a money-sucking monster with extravagant benefits. This would prove to be too costly and hurt in the long run. Now, as then, politicians realize their political success hinges on voting for and keeping the Social Security System intact.

In 1935, the House of Representatives passed the Social Security bill by a vote of 371 to 33. The measure was so popular in the Congress that not long after the law was passed, politicians voted legislation into the agenda that called for increased spending.

Fortunately, some proposed bills were left pending — like the one calling for payments of 40 percent on the first $150 of monthly income for workers over age 65. One Congressman wanted a flat $200 per month for all workers over the age of 60 — a more than 300 percent increase over the benefits voted into the law originally!

Although these bills were defeated, the temptation remains for politicians to try and boost their political status by adding more gravy to the Social Security train.

Any politician who tries to mess with Social Security faces strong opposition from senior citizens. People hate change and are suspicious of any new concept that threatens their sense of security. Even if some bold politician comes up with a better answer to the national retirement problem, as some already have, it will be met with much resistance.

Why? Because monthly checks coming from Uncle Sam are the mainstay of millions of financial diets. The thought of being cut, or the idea of payments not being raised to meet inflation, sends many senior citizens into a panic attack.

This emotional issue also comes with political ramifications. When President Bill Clinton was elected in 1992, he immediately began talking about the reduction of Social Security benefits. As soon as he started reaching into the Social Security cookie jar, he got his hand rapped by a cane. He backed off and stayed away from the subject as George W. Bush has and Barack Obama better do.

The Social Security System desperately needs to be overhauled. If it were managed privately by retirement and investment experts, it would be more profitable. This would keep the government's hand out of the till — which is the reason Social Security is in jeopardy today.

## Social Security - Tax or Retirement Fund?

In 1950, 15 years after payroll withholding began, and 10 years after the first Social Security payments were made, it took 16 active workers paying into the system for each retiree drawing benefits. In early 1996, there were only about five. The projection is that in the year 2020 there will be about 3.5 workers, and in 2030 there will be barely two workers supporting each retiree.

Is the Social Security Tax just another tax? The answers are "Yes" and "No."

If the system doesn't pay off for you, then Social Security is a tax collected from you that benefitted someone else. If, however, the money withheld from your paycheck does pay you benefits at retirement, and those benefits remain at the same proportion as they have in the past, then the system serves as the government intended — as your orchestrated retirement fund.

Social Security is not simply a tax, nor is it only a retirement fund. It acts as both. Social Security withholdings are a tax in the sense that the individual is forced to give the money to the government. Employers are also legally obligated to pay half an employee's Social Security. The program also serves as a retirement fund in the sense that it gives dollars back to an individual at age 62 or 65 or whenever the retiree decides to pull the trigger and receive the benefits.

That presents another question: If it is a retirement fund, is it an efficient form of investing your money as opposed to other retirement vehicles?

In talking to people all over the United States, especially those in the business community, I have found that many think the Social Security System is archaic and should be scrapped altogether. Others, like me, would consider a compromise plan.

Let's consider a few possibilities:

### 1. Opting out.

The government could allow persons to opt out of Social Security if they desire and permit them to invest their dollars into IRAs and other types of savings vehicles.

### 2. Both and,

It has also been suggested that Uncle Sam cut the withholding of Social Security tax from paychecks to half what it is now and allow citizens to fund their own retirement with the other half. To assure that the elderly will have income, the government could require some proof that people are funding another type of retirement savings program in addition to Social Security.

If the Social Security System is being properly funded, and the government is not using the system for purposes other than what it was intended, then why should the government object?

Since Social Security first came into existence, financial advisors have known that properly investing the same dollars in regular investments pays benefits much greater than Social Security ever could. Even knowing this, should the public shy away from Uncle Sam's promises of a pension guarantee funded through Social Security?

Changes in the Social Security System are inevitable. As baby boomers reach retirement age, great pressure will be put on the fund to have the ability to make payments to the recipients. The retirement age will almost certainly have to be raised in order to get more money into the system. In fact, that has already begun.

But is this all bad? People are living longer, so they will need more money than in the past to fund their retirement.

## Planning for Retirement

R. Theodore Benna, author of Escaping the Coming Retirement Crisis and credited with inventing the 401(k) company retirement plan, suggests not counting on Social Security as the sole source of retirement income. He says, in fact, not to count on benefits at all when you are planning your retirement.

In other words, you should plan for your retirement without considering any money coming to you from Social Security. Using this strategy, whether the Social Security System goes broke or not, it will not matter to you. If you do get a monthly check, then it truly will be gravy. There are many books on the market about investing money. My own book, *Put Your Money Where Your Heart Is,* can be bought through www.heritagebuilders.com or www.amazon.com.

If you are nearing retirement age within 10 years, you should expect a substantial decrease in the Social Security benefits now allowed. Why? According to Theodore Benna, death, taxes, and reduced retirement benefits seem virtually certain.

He writes, "Increasing financial pressure to keep the federal bureaucracy afloat will force legislators and other officials to whittle away at Social Security either by raising the retirement age further or by reducing benefits."

You can expect to see more and more changes in the Social Security System.

Rita Koselka, in an article for Forbes magazine, October 9, 1995, titled, *The Legal Ponzi Scheme,* wrote, "When President Clinton pushed his big tax increase through Congress in 1993, 85 percent of a Social Security pension became taxable income to people with substantial amounts of other income. This despite the fact that they had already been taxed on the money they put in. If you have savings and a private pension, the U.S. government taxes your Social Security contributions twice, before they go in and when they come out."

To add insult to injury, the federal government has considered taxing more money going into private pension plans — and the money already socked away into those plans. In addition, many company retirement plans are vastly underfunded and may not be able to pay all the benefits promised to its employees upon retirement. The problem of under funding could catch up with the federal government as well.

How many Americans are worried about their retirement? Not enough of them, according to the Marist College Institute for Public Opinion.

Only 20 percent are worried about making ends meet in the future, and only 35 percent say they sometimes worry. Perhaps most people are counting on the Social Security System to be there when they need it. Sometimes, however, ignorance creates a false sense of security.

Over the years, many people have come to me and asked, "I am putting money aside for retirement, but I don't know if I'll have enough to live on when the time comes or not."

Why are they so uncertain? Because they do not have a financial plan. Like a road map, financial planning shows you where you are right now, and where you are headed in the future, if you stay on track.

## Will the Social Security System Go Broke?

Some economists predict that Social Security will go broke, leaving no retirement for the next generation because the government will default.

I find it hard to believe that the politicians in Washington will allow that to happen. Besides, the government has never defaulted on a Social Security payment nor has one single person ever lost money by investing in government securities. We have no reason to think it will happen now. Major changes are and will be made in the system as we know it today.

In late 1995 and early 1996, unprecedented budget problems emerged from the government. The powerful Contract on America heralded by the Republican House demanded the budget be balanced. Having no choice, President Clinton had reluctantly climbed on the bandwagon. The reason I am reflecting back 14 years is because not much has happened since those historic measures were adopted. Sometimes we forget that decisions made years ago are affecting us now.

When the federal budget gets a truly workable plan, pressure will be put on to downsize money going into entitlements. This pressure will force changes in the Social Security System. Either the government will quit tampering with it, or Congress will come up with a better plan.

Social Security is a political issue. For this reason, no politician will be elected who cannot present a plan that will satisfy the public. As baby boomers are now very close to retirement, overhauling Social Security will become a more volatile issue than ever before.

Not to worry. Social Security will not cease to exist in the near future. Politicians will make sure that all those who have current benefits coming to them are satisfied. To do otherwise would be political suicide. Social Security will be scaled down and revamped so that future generations will live without it. In order for politicians to close out Social Security, they will have to have a plan in place to substitute for it.

Social Security is an entitlement and once people have been used to getting something, they do not want to give it up. Waiting for politicians to take away an entitlement or benefit of the federal government is like waiting for hell to freeze over.

When politicians realize that the Social Security System as we know it now has been a very bad investment for the American people, they will want to improve it the next time around. At the same time, they must make sure Americans have a sensible retirement plan in place that will provide for them in their old age.

In spite of the political maneuvering that will inevitably take place, there is a logical solution to the problem as other nations have discovered.

In the 1970s, Chile's Social Security System went bankrupt. In 1981, Chile's government officials, in trying to come up with a solution to the problem, decided that privatizing the system would be best for the workers of the country.

Here is how this new system works:

1. Every worker in Chile is required to put 10 percent of his earnings into a private pension fund.

2. Private fund managers control the investments although workers can change the allocations in the program if they don't like the returns. Bankers Trust in New York is one of the largest fund managers.

3. Each participant gets a statement every quarter so they can keep up with their earnings in the account.

4. When the retirement age comes, the Chilean worker then takes his money and buys an annuity. Annuities either continue to grow or pay a yearly amount out of the retirement for the rest of the worker's life.

5. In the event the retirement amount falls below the living standard of most Chileans, the Chilean government guarantees the difference.

6. Money not used from the retirement earnings can be passed on to the worker's estate.

Because of Chile's prudence in recognizing the advantage of private funding of a federal retirement law, the savings rate in Chile is among the highest of any nation in the world per capita. The benefits of this kind of social retirement program compared to the Social Security System in the United States are obvious.

Karl Borden, a professor of economics at the University of Nebraska and an expert on the Social Security System, comments on the differences between a social retirement program such as Chile's and America's Social Security System.

Note the critical difference between Chile's system and ours (USA). In ours, your Social Security dollars go to help fund the federal deficit. Thus the only assets of the Social Security trust fund are a lot of federal IOUs. The trust fund invests not a penny in productive assets. The average current return on that federal paper in the trust fund is around eight percent. Had the money been invested in stocks over the past 25 years, the average return would have been more like 11.5 percent, and the pensions would have been far more generous.

Financial advisors and economists have for years agreed that the Social Security System in the United States should be allowed to go to private investment managers. The vast amount of 401(k), 403(b), and other IRA vehicles are invested in a normal diversification of classes of investments made up of market securities, stocks, and bonds as well as some U.S. treasuries, commodities, and cash.

If the federal government would get out of the picture and allow private investment managers to run the system, Americans would end up with a retirement plan that would fund them properly in their golden years. They would no longer have to worry about a government system that has spent all their hard-earned retirement dollars away and have to rely on a part-time income or their personal savings to make ends meet.

## So Long to Sacred Cows

Privatization of the Social Security System is not without problems. Stock market prices rise and fall creating somewhat of a risk to retirees as far as the markets go. Considering, however, the degree of risks involved in privatization versus the risks the government creates, privatization still comes out on top. Why? Because the earnings on the private investment plan would be far more over the same time periods.

Should the system go private? The input of the huge Social Security dollars being invested into American companies would help shore up the nation's economic condition. Investment into America's own businesses rather than financing pet projects of the federal government is a much better choice for this country.

Privatizing the Social Security System would be a good political objective because it would help stimulate the economy. How? By taking away some of the money the federal government spends on entitlements. Entitlements such as Medicaid, Medicare, and Aid to Families with Dependent Children, etc., have grown far bigger than the government ever intended them to be. Of course, any politician who tries to cut or eliminate these entitlements faces strong opposition on many fronts.

If you knew that the money currently taken out of your paycheck and used to fund your Social Security retirement would be worth far more by going to private investors, would you endorse such a plan? Of course you would.

As the public becomes educated on this subject and realizes how privatization would benefit them, they will embrace the idea with open arms.

## "Impossible," You Say?

Other entrenched legislation, like the unpopular 55 mile per hour national speed limit, was repealed. The same will be true of the new tax code laws, a reduction in entitlement programs — and the overhaul of the Social Security System. Some sacred cows just aren't worth the price it takes to keep them alive.

Politicians, however, know that many voters, especially senior citizens, are emotionally attached to Social Security. For that reason, politicians must be forced to bury this archaic system of money laundering. Reform of the Social Security System is an issue that will not go away.

Many ideas will be proposed, and Washington will eventually reform the system. However, do not look for any radical changes to happen quickly.

## The Great Compromise

What would you do if the government announced that anyone paying Social Security taxes could stop and invest the money as they pleased? Many Americans would jump at this opportunity.

How would this great compromise work? Here is a possible plan:

1. Require employers to continue to deduct the required amount of Social Security from employees' pay checks.
2. Allow the deduction to be placed into the hands of a private investment firm.
3. Require reporting from the investment firm along with income tax filing.
4. Allow the payment to be a pre-tax deduction.
5. Allow the person to contribute more than the standard deduction if he so chooses.

When Americans save money, the nation as a whole always benefits. Although many facets affect our economic livelihood, and many changes need to be made in our country, we cannot continue to throw our money down this governmental sink hole. The Social Security System demands attention.

## Bleeding the Elderly Dry

A gentleman whose 88 -year-old mother is in a nursing home told me, "Because she had a lot of money, my mother could not qualify for certain government benefits for the elderly such as Medicare. Now the nursing home where she lives takes more than $3000 of her income per month. They have almost bled her dry."

Other seniors who have no money are living just as well on government assistance and haven't given a dime of their own money to support themselves. Something is wrong with this picture.

I am in favor of giving the elderly all they need, and God blesses this nation for taking care of its aged. But I am against penalizing someone because they have been diligent all their lives, saved their money, worked for it, and then have to lose it because the government doesn't believe they deserve the same treatment as someone without money.

This whole situation was created by money, or the lack of it. It all revolves around the dollar just like most other circumstances in our lives, and this is something that will never change unless we elect politicians that have American citizens and not themselves at heart. Every year, new politicians enter politics, win races, and end up in our nation's Capitol for the first time only to be eaten by the sharks that are entrenched in the control panel of the nation's switches.

My friend ran for public office for the first time. He is a Christian. He was elected to Congress and hated it. He spent two years there and then ran for Governor of his state and won the election. In both places, he found himself surrounded by incumbents whom had been there for so many years, they controlled everything and everybody. You either played by their rules, or you would find yourself on the outskirts of the Capitol looking in.

The only way to stop this nonsense is term limits. The people of America need to push for this immediately and allow a Senator no more than 12 years in Congress, and a House Representative a maximum of 8 years.

"But," you say, "no one will run for government because of the expense and limitations." That's what the politicians want you to believe. No, what will happen is the pundits will be gone, and the statesmen will take over. Men and women will come out of the woodwork who have the money to serve the country and the country's interest instead of their own. Businessmen will run for office and would be elected, and the lawyers will be gone except for those who have legitimate careers and will take time off to help run the government.

What does this sidebar have to do with Social Security? Throwing the politicians in the Potomac River who have been running us in the ground (and the red) will save the country financially and put us on the right track. Social Security will get healthy, and our life of contributing to this retirement tax won't be lost.

In summary, I do not believe the Social Security is going into oblivion never to be seen again. Why? Because no politician is going back to the Capitol if that happens on his/her watch, including the President. That is why they will keep it reasonably healthy if not fix it entirely.

# CHAPTER EIGHT

## FACE TO FACE WITH THE IRS

"If 10% is good enough for God, it should be good enough for the IRS."

Profound words from a bumper sticker I once saw on the back of an old pickup truck. It's my favorite because that simple statement reveals how people feel about the IRS.

No other organization connected to the federal government generates more hatred than the Internal Revenue Service. Anything connected with the IRS brings an assault of deadly language, oaths, and vows. IRS agents are despised although most are regular people just doing their jobs. Still the stigma goes with the territory, and every IRS agent knows from the start that he will be subject to the public's disdain.

Like the German Gestapo or the Soviet KGB, the mere mention of the IRS creates fear and trembling in even the most honest, upstanding citizen.

I used to work for a company with the unfortunate name National Revenue, although it often worked to my advantage.

When calling on a potential client, I first had to get past gate keepers, security guards, and receptionists. I would slow down my speech and say very distinctly, "Tell him that National Revenue is here to see him."

Almost invariably, eyebrows were raised and in hushed tones, the question was asked, "The Internal Revenue?"

The hearer was responding, as most people do, in fear to the word REVENUE.

After I explained I was not from the Internal Revenue Service, an audience with the potential client was quickly granted. The relief was somewhat like a finger that just stopped hurting after being hit with a hammer.

Certain groups believe that the IRS was illegally established in the first place and is illegal today. Others consider the government's initial need for a bureaucratic tax collector as essential but think the IRS has stepped beyond the bounds of its reason for existence. I agree with this second opinion.

The tax codes in this country are too many and too costly, making it nearly impossible for most CPAs, tax lawyers, and financial advisors to keep up with the ever-changing tax laws. Firms, such as the one I used to own, do a lot of financial planning, and keeping on top of the latest changes in the tax code has become a monumental chore.

## Crocodiles on the Amazon

Simply getting a threatening letter from the IRS can be intimidating, to say the least. The pressure cooker of bankruptcy court pales in comparison to the stress and tension of dealing with the Internal Revenue Service. Believe me, I know from personal experience.

At one point, I was repeatedly called into the offices of the IRS because they didn't believe the amount of my church contributions. With receipts in hand, it was easy to prove that I did indeed give to my church on a regular basis every Sunday. After a few years of being called in to prove this, they finally left me alone on that matter.

The IRS can be so intimidating that some of my associates encouraged me not to write this chapter but to let "the sleeping dog lie." This, however, is my opportunity to vent.

When I left the family construction business in Kentucky, I needed the help of a CPA to settle my affairs and finalize my business activities. I had sold some equipment at a loss, so my CPA took the loss as a deduction from my taxes.

After four years or so, I got a letter from the IRS saying that I owed a certain amount of money, and if I didn't pay it, they were going to take my first born son. I was also invited to have a meeting with one of their agents should I have any questions.

At that time, I didn't know that certain professionals are certified to practice before the IRS and that I wouldn't even have to appear but could send someone in my place. Today, I don't care what it costs, I always send my accountant who is an Enrolled Agent and can practice before the IRS. This has relieved stress for me on more than one occasion.

In the intervening years, I had moved out of state, and my CPA had died. His wife had also passed away, and his daughter, who had worked in his office and might know the whereabouts of the records, had married, moved out of the area, and was nowhere to be found. I was in a pickle. The IRS was saying I owed more than $15,000 on a $7,500 deduction, and I was terrified.

I had just moved to California, was working on my doctorate, and was more or less cash poor. There was nothing left for me to do except lay prostrate before them and hope to work out a solution to the problem.

Although I am not easily intimidated, I don't remember being more overwhelmed with anxiety than the day of my meeting with the IRS. As a college student in Brazil, I had faced angry crocodiles on the Amazon River and at the moment I walked into the IRS office, even that seemed like a pleasant experience.

First of all, this was in the early 1980s, and the IRS was bogged down in frustrating cases. As a result, agents had little patience with anyone who questioned their policies. Approaching them with meekness and humility didn't work either; you were still treated like the second-class citizen they think you are.

Being led down the long corridor of IRS offices is worse than facing a Nazi interrogation. At any time, you expect someone from behind a closed door to scream out in pain as rubber hoses are slashed across their foreheads. My thought was I would be put in a chair, bound, a large lamp would be shone in my face, and they would prod information from me with a bare electric cord.

## Legalized Extortion

Although my IRS agent turned out to be a small black lady instead of the Gestapo-like figure I had expected, that didn't lessen my anxiety.

"The final tally after penalties and interest is $29,000, Mr. Smith," she said, looking me up and down. "How are you going to take care of this?"

That was almost twice as much money as I had been led to believe I owed in the first place. My blood pressure must have been at its highest as the frustration and anger surged up and down my body.

"I don't have that kind of money!" I exclaimed loudly. "I can't pay this bill!"

"How much can you pay?" she asked.

"You mean there is a possibility that I can pay less?" I answered rather dismayed.

It was then and there that I learned that IRS agents can do just about anything they want, for anybody they want, for any amount they want, any time they want.

The agent explained, "You can compromise with us if you can prove that this tax liability is going to be a hardship on you."

"Well it is," I replied, somewhat irritated.

She left the room and brought me some forms. As I began to look them over, I realized I would need every ounce of the education I was earning as a Ph.D. to be able to fill out the paperwork.

"Look, I just got a new job as a stockbroker, and my career is going to take some time to get off the ground. I am struggling building my business," I explained, hoping for a reprieve.

This narrative had little effect on the agent because she looked me over and replied, "You can afford to pay the bill Mr. Smith because as a stockbroker, you are going to make lots of money."

Apparently she had dealt with stockbrokers before.

Now what was I to do? Every time I felt I could get to her, she cut my legs out from under me.

It was time to make an emotional appeal. "Are you a Christian?" I asked.

Now, I have no idea where that question came from or why I

asked it, but for some reason I felt if she knew that I was a moral, upstanding person, she would have more compassion.

Curtly she responded, "We're here to interview you."

There is nothing you can do with the belligerent IRS when they get the upper hand. I did successfully convince her that I could only pay $1,000 at the time, and a monthly payment plan would be appreciated.

She then sought a supervisor who agreed to approve the plan immediately if I could write a check for $1,000 on the spot.

I said, "I left my checkbook in the car."

"When you return, we'll let you know how much the monthly payment will be," they said, obviously convinced I would not try to escape.

To add insult to injury, I discovered in my nervousness I had locked my keys in my car. I had to wait until a locksmith came, and charged me an arm and a leg, to write a check to keep the pit bulls from chewing off my legs.

## The Reign of Terror

I signed the compromise, wrote the check, and was then told, "Do not be late with your payment or all compromises are off. You will have to pay the debt immediately, or we will seize all your assets and attach your wages."

I spent the next 24 months paying off the debt at $1,500 per month. In other words, I had to make it at my profession or suffer bank liens, property liens, and other forms of harassment the IRS would inflict on me in order to carry out their promises.

I believe in paying my just debts, but I don't believe in legalized extortion.

I later learned why they were so anxious to settle into a payment plan. Because I was easy. In other words, they knew they had me scared, so they took advantage of me. I also learned, or at least was told, that the agents get a percentage of the payoff they squeeze out of their fellow citizens.

While once intimidated, I was not anymore. The IRS does have limits, and certain laws protect the taxpayer. If you understand that the IRS has to abide by those laws and that as a taxpayer you have rights, dealing with the IRS can be a far less-frightening experience.

In recent years, the IRS is trying to improve its image — and for good reason. A day is coming when there won't be any need for IRS audits or for IRS workers because there won't be an IRS.

Before too long, a conservative Congress or scared Democrats will give us sweeping tax reforms that will revolutionize the way we finance our government. Those revisions will be the forerunner of the abolition of the Internal Revenue Service.

Until that happens, there are a few things you can do to lessen the pressure in dealing with the IRS while we are in the final days of their reign of terror.

## The Power to Harass

Throughout history, countries that employed collectors to bring in tax dollars created ill will among the public. Why? Because of the awesome power tax collectors exercise aver the people.

In Bible times, tax collectors were not only feared but were mistrusted and considered criminals. Why? Because they inflated the taxes and kept the difference for themselves. Everyone knew this and hated them for it. Tax collectors had authority over the common folk, but they abused that power. One tax collector, after becoming a follower of Jesus Christ, offered to give back what he had wrongfully taken from the poor.

We, American's, have been living with the feelings of ill will since our ancestors migrated west in the 1700s.

Our Nation's Revolutionary War was fought for two main reasons:

1. **Freedom of worship.**
2. **Freedom from heavy taxation imposed by the British government.**

Before the war, taxation was so great that a statement in the Declaration of Independence indicates that the King of Britain "has erected a multitude of new offices, and sent hither swarms of officers to harass our people, and eat out their substance."

The Internal Revenue Service of the United States has this same kind of power and even more. Although they must abide by certain laws, they still abuse their authority over America's citizens. Certain IRS powers, however, can be challenged constitutionally.

Still, no other agency of the United States can operate so independently while ignoring congressional authority.

Congressman George Hansen, in his publication, *To Harass Our People, The IRS and Government Abuse of Power,* lists the unique powers granted, or assumed, by the IRS:

- Only the IRS can attach 100 percent of a tax debtor's wages and/or property.
- Only the IRS can invade the privacy of a citizen without court process of any kind.
- Only the IRS can seize property without a court order.
- Only the IRS can force a citizen to try his case in a special court governed by the IRS.
- Only the IRS can compel production of documents, records, and other materials without a court case being in existence.
- Only the IRS can with impunity publish a citizen's debt to the IRS.
- Only the IRS can legally, without a court order, subject citizens to electronic surveillance.
- Only the IRS can force waiver of the Statue of Limitations and other citizen rights through power of arbitrary assessment.
- Only the IRS uses extralegal coercion. Threats to witnesses to examine their taxes regularly produce whatever evidence the IRS dictates.
- Only the IRS is free to violate a written agreement with a citizen.
- Only the IRS uses reprisals against citizens and public officials alike.
- Only the IRS can take property on the basis of conjecture.
- Only the IRS is free to maintain lists of citizens guilty of no crime for the purpose of monitoring them.
- Only the IRS envelops all citizens.
- Only the IRS publicly admits that its purpose is to instill fear into the citizenry as a technique of performing its function.

I am not an extremist on this issue, nor am I unrealistic. There are some things the IRS cannot do, and the citizen has power over them. The limitations of the IRS are not widely known, and few people know how to exercise their rights as a citizen over them. The IRS must abide by the law, and if they are out of bounds, they can be called on the issues and forced to obey.

## Bureaucratic Vampirism

Prior to 1913, the United States had no income tax. When the Sixteenth Amendment allowed the first income taxes, it only applied to the wealthiest people. In fact, only 12 percent of the population initially paid income taxes.

By the early 1940s, these figures doubled but still only 25 percent of the population paid income tax according to the Sixteenth Amendment. It is interesting to note how this income tax was paid. The person paying the tax deducted his tax at the end of the year. Most paid around 10 percent of their income. Each person had the responsibility of determining their own taxes and writing the government a check. There was no withholding, and all payments were more or less voluntary.

When did taxes become mandatory? With the passage of the Social Security Act in 1935. This was the first forcible tax and involuntary assessment on the income of the American people. In other words, pay the tax or else!

The Social Security Tax led to withholding income tax as we know it today. Mandatory tax was withheld from each pay check, or mandatory estimated payments were to be made by independent business people.

Enter the Internal Revenue Service, which suddenly became powerful by design. The more people paying income tax the greater the demands by government to see the taxes were being paid.

This led to more rules for collecting those taxes until we now have a Pandora's Box of confusing regulations that not even the IRS can sort out. The income tax rules are so extensive and complicated that no one person can understand or interpret them all. The forcible collection of these taxes created a vast agency now embroiled in bureaucratic vampirism of the American people.

What is the answer to this blood-sucking dilemma? Do away with the IRS altogether, and its demise may come sooner than we think. In the meantime, reform of some kind is on the way.

According to recent polls, more than 66 percent of Americans indicate they are fed up with the system. As a result, IRS reform will be a huge political election issue in upcoming years.

Shirley Peterson, a former IRS Commissioner, said, "We should repeal the Internal Revenue Code and start over."

My intention is not to offend those friends of mine at the Internal Revenue Service, nor to slight the honesty of the thousands of employees who earn their living by working for the IRS. My beef is with the governmental bureaucracy that has allowed the IRS to grow into an unrestrained monster allowed to prey on hard-working Americans.

Even the liberal *New York Times* in writing about the Sixteenth Amendment at its inaugural in 1913 said, "When men get in the habit of helping themselves to the property of others, they cannot be easily cured of it." They may have been quoting Thomas Jefferson who said something similar a hundred years before.

Raymond Keating of the Small Business Survival Foundation points out: "Between 1913 and 1994, inflation-adjusted federal government expenditures increased by 13,592 percent!" That figure could be extrapolated even more considering another 15 years have gone by since Mr. Keating figured this out.

Columnist Joseph Sobran writes in his March 17, 1996, column that "the debasement of the dollar has long since made tax serfs of the middle class, as inflation has moved everyone into higher brackets, And so today's citizens find themselves not only taxed at levels their ancestors would have considered outrageous, but also bearing a colossal debt of $5 trillion." In 1966!

The average citizen in 1913 paid zero federal income tax; this generation pays *at least* 28 percent. Before Ronald Reagan hailed the liberal-Congress-taxing-Americans to the hilt and reined them in, taxes were much higher. Add to that 15.3 percent in Social Security and Medicare; about 3 plus percent for state taxes; 1 plus percent for local taxes; and your state's sales tax (if it has one) — and you're paying nearly 50 percent of your income in taxes!

# The IRS Face Lift

Recently, the IRS suspended its most dreaded audit program, the Taxpayer Compliance Measurement Program (TCMP). These audits allow IRS representatives to finely comb through a person's financial records looking for persons to target.

Let's look at some of the guidelines used for the TCMP scrutiny. Each taxpayer must prove every item on their return. Part of the requirement includes producing a marriage license to prove they are indeed entitled to a joint return and birth certificates for the children to prove the deduction taken for each child.

The audit is so extensive that it has caused psychological trauma in many of the victims. One doctor said, "The TCMP audit is an autopsy without the benefit of dying."

In an effort to clean up its act, the IRS is making its offices and officers more "user friendly" by adding more finesse and less intimidation. They have finally realized that scaring people to death does not enhance their image. Voters need to put more pressure on Congress to insist that the IRS develop more humane practices and compassionate attitudes.

From four pages of the first 1040 Form to the more than 40,000 pages of tax form instructions, billions of man hours are needed to solve the income tax problems the Internal Revenue Service has created. No wonder everyone stays in a constant state of confusion.

It is nearly impossible for anyone to do their taxes alone. It takes the expertise of a CPA who constantly educates himself just to keep up with the changes. Since 1986, there have been thousands of changes in the tax code, causing the chaos and confusion. Even Lloyd Bentsen, once Chairman of the Tax Committee and responsible for writing some of the tax laws, had an outside CPA firm do his taxes.

In its quest to "serve" the American people, the IRS gives tax advice; but I don't recommend calling them because one third of their answers are wrong, and that could cost you money. The IRS now has a disclaimer concerning any advice given over the phone.

In his book, *Costly Returns,* economist James L. Payne does an outstanding job of analyzing the IRS fiasco and points out this amazing statistic: "Of the tax dollars collected, 65 percent of those dollars collected are spent to collect the dollars!"

Imagine the impact this has on the economy. Erroneous liens, penalties, and levies have emaciated thousands of American households unnecessarily; making them victims of this many-tentacled Gargantuan we call the IRS.

## The Dangling Corpse

A Forbes magazine article, We May Not Catch You, But If We Do written by Laura Sanders, notes, "The IRS can't do a lot of audits. It makes up for that by scaring the pants off under-payers with hefty penalties."

Penalties are used to punish the taxpayer and make him an example for all other taxpayers who consider cheating on their taxes. That is why you need someone qualified to do your taxes.

When the IRS discovers you owe back taxes, there are all kinds of consequences, like negligence penalties, underpayment of tax penalties (these can be severe), interest on unpaid tax, and interest on all the penalties.

The IRS can bankrupt you — but filing for bankruptcy will not exempt you from your IRS debt. Those doomed to the IRS prison of tax obligation will likely die before they escape.

A Tax Letter by CPA Firm Jensen and Wiggins, St. Helena, California, gives the following breakdown of the penalty situation:

"There are over 100 penalties at the IRS's disposal. Tax penalties generate $4 billion annually. In addition to penalties, the IRS charges interest on late payment of taxes."

The penalties most often assessed against individuals are:

1. **The Underestimation Penalty**
2. **The Failure-to-File Penalty**
3. **The Failure-to-Pay Penalty**

With the Underestimation Penalty, the IRS charges the taxpayer the interest (at the IRS's rates) that's due on the amount of the estimated tax shortage for the period during which it remains unpaid.

The Failure-to-File Penalty is assessed when the taxpayer does not file the return on time. The IRS charges the taxpayer 5% of the tax due per month, with a maximum of 25% of the tax.

The Failure-to-Pay Penalty is assessed when the taxpayer fails to pay tax on time. The IRS charges the taxpayer 5% of the tax due per month, with a maximum of 25% of the tax. This penalty doesn't apply for any month during which the Failure- to-Pay penalty applies.

Other penalties commonly assessed are the Negligence Penalty and the Substantial Understatement Penalty. For these penalties the IRS charges taxpayers 20% of the additional tax that is due to the negligence or understatement.

"Negligence" means the taxpayer hasn't kept the proper records, hasn't complied with the tax rules, hasn't substantiated items that need to be substantiated, or has otherwise been careless in preparing the return.

"Substantial Understatement" means the taxpayer's real tax (as claimed by the IRS) is at least 10% more than what he or she has shown on the return, or is at least $5,000 more than what is shown on the return, whichever of these is greater.

On the higher end of the penalty scale are the Civil Fraud penalties, which can be double or triple the amounts assessed for the Negligence Penalty. Finally, the criminal penalties carry the heaviest sanctions.

Anyone who has a problem paying his taxes obviously has a problem financially. No one wants to pay a penalty of any kind, and penalties should not be so small that they are of no consequence to the taxpayer. However, a penalty is a penalty.

Some IRS agents hate to collect certain penalties because of their unnecessary severity. As these brutal penalties accumulate, they leave little opportunity for those at the mercy of the IRS to recover. The sheer force of these outrageous penalties has driven many businesses into bankruptcy.

The IRS should ease up on American citizens (except for fraud, which should carry heavy penalties). The U.S. Government should not rely on penalties for tax revenue.

Laura Sanders writes: "The IRS technique is like the deterrent against crime used in the Middle Ages." After hanging a culprit, they would leave the corpse dangling in the town square for a few days as a warning to others. A way of saying, "we may not catch you stealing, but if we do, look where you will end up."

Because of my background, counseling as part of my job at my church brings many people living in the pressure cooker to see me for advice. Oftentimes, these counseling sessions deal with the problems being created in businesses by the IRS.

"She's absolutely terrified," our senior pastor said during an appointment to jointly speak with a distressed member of our congregation.

"You are obviously stressed more than anyone I have dealt with for a long time," I explained as the agony on this lady's face was apparent as she nervously sat across my desk. "Tell me what is causing this cumbersome load you are carrying."

"I am afraid of the IRS," she said.

"What are you afraid of?" I asked with much concern.

"I'm afraid they will take me to jail," she answered.

After a series of questions as to what the nature of her fear was, I asked if she could afford an attorney I would recommend who was an expert in delinquent tax matters. She was able to pay a certain amount, so I made the call and asked that my attorney friend take this case.

A very common offense in the United States is to pay employees in cash without really thinking about the consequences. This is against the law, but lay business people may not be aware of this, so they continue the practice. This person had reason for concern because it is actually fraud not to withhold proper taxes from a person's wages and pay them in cash.

None of this was this woman's fault as she had inherited the situation. I felt it necessary that she face the IRS with this situation before they discovered the errors and made a violent move against her. An attorney in the presence was a must not only for expert negotiations but to keep the client from divulging any material statements that could be used against her.

Almost immediately, she felt relief. As it turned out, she did not need to pay an attorney. The IRS has a "Safe Harbor Rule" that can be used one time to avoid criminal fraud or intent when the tax is paid.

I have counseled with people who have been years in these kinds of situations and live in constant fear that at any moment their house is going to be torn down by the IRS. In one case, the distressed man was a farm worker in the mountains of Kentucky and did not have a Social Security number and never paid a tax of any kind. He relied on his employers to pay cash and keep their mouths shut. He lived in his own pressure cooker, with no relief from the stress. He confessed and, in the end, the case was settled without criminal trial.

The very best offense, if anyone reading this book has a problem the Internal Revenue Service will eventually discover, is to go talk to them about it. You will find in most cases they do not want to put you in jail and will resolve the case. The IRS also cannot do things to you that are beyond the limit of the law. They can seize assets, they can lien bank accounts, but that is not the end of your life. They will work with you as they did with me.

Today, there are many organizations that will help you settle your tax situations without costly attorney bills. In most cases, they will negotiate on your behalf and save thousands less than you would have paid the IRS by trying to settle yourself, including their fees. I highly recommend that you do not try to face these people by yourself without proper representation.

When an attorney or Enrolled Agent operates on your behalf, all liens and threats of liens immediately stop; no seizures can take place after notice that someone is negotiating for you, and the IRS cannot threaten you or levy your bank account.

Remember, when the IRS is on the prowl, they don't care if you can't pay your tithes or you have outstanding checks that are going to bounce when the money is missing. There are more than 140 civil penalties the IRS can throw at an individual. In most cases, the penalties and interest far exceed the amount of tax owed.

## Fighting Back

I have been audited several times. At first, I thought the IRS was simply trying to get me.

Almost every time I was called in for the audit, I was asked to produce records. Keeping good records saved my neck. Most of the audits were due to the charitable contributions I make to my church and others. My giving was sometimes so substantial the IRS would not believe it. (I don't say this to brag; I am grateful to have had the opportunity to give and be blessed).

How can you protect yourself in case of an audit? Here are some suggestions:

1. Keep records of expenses for several years in files. One of the best investments I ever made as a young man was buying a filing cabinet.

2. A letter from the church or non-profit organization, which verifies your contributions, should be attached to your record of giving. You must have a receipt for any single contribution over $250. Canceled checks alone are no longer valid since people sometimes cash checks at church or write checks to the church for things other than contributions.

3. Keep a log of expenses. This takes a little discipline but will pay off in the long run. Back up the log with receipts.

4. Keep receipts to verify expenses if you are self-employed. After my first IRS audit, I learned the importance of getting receipts as proof of payment. Even if you owe no income tax, you have to pay 14 cents on every dollar to Social Security up to your limit.

5. If required to go for an audit, take your CPA with you or an Enrolled Agent who can go in your place and appear at the audit. This can be expensive but will probably save money — and stress — in the long run. The IRS can require that you be present, but they must issue a summons to do so; but more than likely, they won't.

6. You always have the option of making the IRS go to court. Going this route can work for or against you. On the positive side, it makes the IRS auditors nervous; especially, if they know they don't have a hard case against you. Many dollars are lost each year because the person being audited allows the IRS to assess them without challenge. On the down side, if the IRS does take you to court, be prepared to pay a lot of money. IRS court cases are very expensive.

7. Don't volunteer information that has nothing to do with the audit. The IRS often goes on fishing expeditions designed to prove you have neglected your taxes on purpose. I once read that IRS agents will ask about your educational background to prove you were smart enough to know what you were doing and then file a fraudulent case against you.

8. You can stop the IRS from auditing you year after year for the same reason. After three audits to make me prove my church contributions, they stopped. The IRS has rules against repeat audits.

9. You don't have to allow the IRS to come to your personal premises. You can refuse this intrusion. You can also refuse to be harassed by an agent who wants to see every little detail of your records. You can insist he "spot check," and if he or she won't cooperate, you can end the audit and file a complaint.

10. You can have your attorney present if the IRS wants to interview any of your employees.

## Probing Questions

In Forbes magazine, October 9, 1995, Laura Sanders and Janet Novack's article, *Knowing When to Say No,* included a list of questions the IRS may ask in an effort to probe into your personal business at an audit. Note that some of these questions have nothing to do with an audit:

1. Home phone number.
2. Work phone.
3. Birth date
4. Confirmation that previous year is on extension. Copy must be provided.
5. Either spouse previously married? Paying alimony or receiving? If so, how much and to whom paid?
6. Educational background of both spouses; highest degree received.
7. Taxpayer's previous occupation, employer, and date.
8. Date of birth of children.
9. Purchase documents; application; closing documents for home. Mortgage holder? Payment amount?
10. Other real estate owned and when it was acquired? Monthly rent? Do you manage or do you have a management company?
11. Did you make any improvements during tax year in question to your real estate?

12. How many autos do you own? What are they? What is the payment?

13. Do you own any large assets (over $10,000) besides auto and real estate?

14. Did you sell any assets in tax year in question? If so, what, to whom and for how much?

15. Did you loan anyone any money during tax year in question?

16. Did you receive repayments of any loaned money in tax year in question?

17. What loans do you have besides auto and mortgage? How much? Monthly payments?

18. Do you ever take cash advances from credit cards or lines of credit? How much and how often?

19. What cash did you have on hand in tax year in question, usually have on hand, personally or business, not in a bank; at your home, safe deposit box, hidden somewhere, etc?

20. What is the largest amount of cash you had at any one time in tax year in question?

21. Did you transfer funds between your accounts? If so, how much and when?

22. Did your spouse deposit his/her paychecks into the bank? What account?

23. Did you ever redeposit funds previously withdrawn from your accounts?

24. Do you have a safe deposit box? Where? What's in it?

25. Were you involved in any cash transactions of $10,000 or more?

26. How long has your business been at its current location? Where was it previously?

27. Employee business expenses — what meals are being deducted? Please provide appointment calendar, receipts, business purpose, and business relationships for all expenses.

More than 200 years ago, John Marshall prophetically said, "The power of tax is the power to destroy."

This is another reason the IRS needs to be abolished.

It is time for tax reform in the United States. Let's look at some changes that would be positive for the American people.

## The Flat Tax

It appears that major reforms in the IRS code are inevitable. It will be a campaign issue in coming elections until the constituency that opposes the IRS, which is most of the American public, gets what it wants.

The massive IRS, and the bureaucracy necessary to run it, strangles the American people. Who doesn't want to reduce the IRS or get rid of it altogether?

"If 10 percent is good enough for God, it should be good enough for the IRS." (Some are now proposing that 17 percent is good enough.)

California Assemblymen, Arthur Laffer, Victor Canto, and Howard Kaloagian initiated a flat tax proposal for the state of California in the mid-1990s which reads:

"The premise is simple: taxes should not be social engineering tools with which to punish or reward certain behavior or to redistribute resources. In order to preserve personal liberty and promote economic prosperity, taxes should be levied at the lowest possible rate and on the broadest possible base — but at a rate equal for everyone."

It is not right to punish people who make more money than others with higher taxes. This is socialism, and if we all think about it for awhile, we'll realize we don't want socialism. Slowly we have let the government reward people for being dysfunctional instead of helping them with the problems. Flat tax, although not perfect, will eliminate a lot of unnecessary loopholes, eliminate other taxes, and create a much-needed slimming down of the Internal Revenue Service.

Under the flat tax, a business or corporation can simply state its revenue, subtract its allowable deductions, total what's left and pay the tax. This can all be done on a form no bigger than a 3" X 5" index card.

## Objections to the Flat Tax

Why do I and other financial professionals recommend an overhaul in the tax system? Because the entire tax structure is out of control.

In 1988, when former California governor Jerry Brown proposed a flat tax, not too many people were paying attention. If some of Jerry Brown's other views weren't so eccentric, the flat tax issue would now be a reality.

It is hard to imagine that anyone would oppose the flat tax proposals, but many politicians do. Why? Because they are comfortable with the status-quo and don't want to rock the bureaucratic boat.

Opponents of the flat tax have five main objections. Let's consider these and sort out the truth from the fiction.

### 1. Many Americans will get a free ride at the expense of others.

That is already true. Many Americans are getting a free ride now through entitlement programs that should have been done away with ages ago. This is part of the overall problem. Our government funds too many social programs that are destroying the nation, not helping it.

Welfare recipients are one example. With certain welfare spending there is no incentive to work. The fear that Americans will take the new tax relief as an incentive to become more burdensome to the government is ridiculous. Under our present tax system, too many free-loaders are already taking advantage of taxpayers.

### 2. Taxes will be raised on the middle class.

Taxes will not be raised on the middle class. The flat tax proposal is a tax cut from 39 percent to 17 percent, and the first $36,000 of income is exempt from any tax. With a deduction for each child, most middle class people will pay far less income tax than they do now.

### 3. A flat tax will allow lower income people to get off without paying taxes.

One of the complaints by many liberals is that we don't do enough for the poorer people of the country. What better way to help poorer people escape certain poverty than to get them off the relief programs that drive the taxes the rest of us pay higher and higher?

Giving the poor a tax break leaves them with more money to spend and enables them to move off welfare, get a job, and improve their lifestyle. With less of their money going to the government, they have more money to put into the economy.

**4. Richer people would not have as much tax to pay as they do now.**

So what? No matter what tax laws are in effect, the rich have always been able to find tax loopholes. And if they can't, they move to the Riviera and spend their money in foreign economies and stop investing in America.

If they feel the flat tax is fair, the rich will pay the taxes and invest in our economy — not Europe's. This creates jobs for Americans.

And who knows? After their tax shelters are exercised by the flat tax, the rich may actually end up putting more revenue into the tax system than they do now. Trying to punish the rich in this nation is like shooting yourself in both feet.

**5. The middle class will lose the mortgage deduction on their homes.**

Under the present tax system, I have given up or severely taken a cut in almost every deduction previously allowed to American taxpayers. My home is the only good thing left I can deduct. However, I will gladly give up my mortgage interest deduction to save 22 percent on my tax bill.

What about senior citizens and home owners whose houses are paid off and who no longer qualify for a mortgage deduction? Are we going to penalize them? What about people who choose to rent? Wouldn't it be fairer to eliminate the home mortgage deduction and lower everyone's taxes?

## The Consumption Tax

Another revolutionary proposal - the consumption tax - would eliminate the Internal Revenue Service entirely. Why? Because we wouldn't need it anymore.

The consumption tax is simply a national sales tax on purchases. When you buy something you pay tax on the item, and that money goes to finance government services.

This simple proposal would eliminate complicated withholding procedures that cost businesses hundreds of millions of dollars in personnel and accounting fees. No more looming April 15th and other dreaded filing dates.

Although I hope this is the direction the nation takes, I don't believe it will happen before a flat tax is in place. As the forerunner of tax code revolution, the flat tax will lead to the initiation of the National Consumption Tax and eventually the abolition of the IRS.

*I get excited just thinking about it!*

As people realize that the more they spend the more they have to pay, they will be more careful about what they buy. This new incentive will launch a great savings boom in the country. This will result in several positive outcomes:

1. Tax shelters would be eliminated.

2. Income from investments would no longer be taxed.

3. The doomsayers' fears that the country is broke would be expelled.

4. Fraud from unreported income would be eliminated.

5. The estimated $300 billion to $600 billion in annual IRS costs to assure compliance with the tax laws could be put to better use.

6. Instead of 114 million individual tax returns, only 15 million retailers would have to file.

7. Congress will be forced to stop unnecessary spending.

Wouldn't certain programs, like Medicaid and Medicare, that we now fund as a nation suffer? Not if Congress is forced to cut spending on some entitlements and other specially funded projects that are wasting billions of taxpayer dollars. If our elected representatives get into more sensible spending programs, the national entitlements that are necessary will survive because there will be plenty of money.

In his April 15, 1996 column titled, *Abolish the IRS with a National Retail Sales Tax,* Don Feder notes, "Certain Safeguards are crucial. Simultaneous with a national retail sales taxes enactment, the Sixteenth Amendment to the Constitution which permits an individual income tax, would have to be repealed."

That's for sure! The last thing we need is a national sales tax plus a return to the individual income tax!

## Why We Need Drastic Tax Reform

Very few, if any Americans alive, can remember when our nation had no income tax. Believe it or not, this country operated very well without an income tax for most of its history and can do so again.

What is the purpose of taxes? To raise revenue for genuine government expenditures. Right? Unfortunately, this has not been and is not now the case.

Big, centralized government has misused the tax base of the American public. Almost no one — except the liberals in Congress — agree with the spending procedures of the government in the past 30 or so years. The huge deficits we now face have been created by policy makers who wantonly spend our money.

What is the best way to reverse the big-spending trend in Washington? Give them less money. This will force them to use our tax dollars for legitimate programs that benefit Americans over all.

In the pressure cooker of life, government policies create unnecessary financial problems for many Americans and provide little relief in solving social problems. While there are no simple solutions, one major change would alleviate many of our economic and social problems.

What is that change? To reform the tax codes. This will spur on business, bring foreign investors back to America, and allow the lifestyle of the American people to improve.

Can you imagine what would happen if our government initiated a flat tax or a consumption tax? No longer strapped by burdensome income and business taxes, we could begin to invest in our country and its people.

*Reducing taxes will not eliminate the primary problem.*

To appease the public, however, short-sighted politicians who oppose the flat tax suggest instead a reduction in taxes. That tactic does not eliminate the major problem.

Americans have had tax deductions before only to find them rendered useless by big spenders like the liberal Democrats and presidents who raised taxes. Even President George H. Bush raised taxes and killed the 12-year boom the Reagan Administration gave us by cutting taxes. That is one major reason he lost the election to William J. Clinton.

Every presidential administration dickers with the income tax, raising and lowering and using new tax proposals as a platform. We need drastic reforms that will work in any administration, making it impossible for presidents or Congress to change the tax code, so they can have more of our money to spend on frivolous, pork-barrel projects.

This brings us to why we need a balanced budget amendment. Such a law would require Congress to keep spending within the limits of a proposed budget. A mandatory balanced budget is crucial to making tax reform work.

The ball is now in our court. American voters have the power to insist that our elected officials - from the President on down — initiate tax reform and balance the budget.

All this may seem out of place in a book like this one. We have just experienced one of the most historic elections in our nation by electing our first black President. Sadly, this President does not hold dear those beliefs of Christian Black America I grew up with and have known all my life. For this reason, I somehow believe that God will humble us by this current deep recession; the President and his liberal Congress will fail; and He will raise up the person who will stand once again for the freedoms and doctrines we all hold dear.

# CHAPTER NINE

# NO TIME TO PANIC!

Take a look at some of the book titles on the shelves in 1998 and 1999.

- *Surviving in an Underground Economy*
- *Bankruptcy 1995*
- *The Coming Economic Earthquake*
- *Crisis Investing*
- *The Great Depression of 1990*
- *Whatever Happened to The American Dream?*
- *Storm Shelter*
- *The Hyperinflation Survival Guide*
- *End Times Digest*
- *The Plague of the Black Debt*
- *The Millennium Bug*

This sampling of negative doomsayer books reminds me of Chicken Little and his fear-based news bulletin, "The sky is falling!" Yet, most of these books were written by Christian authors.

At this writing, we are in a deep recession that could end up being the worse the nation has ever experienced, and the influx of recent doom and gloom prognosticators has convinced Americans our nation will self-destruct. Such fatalistic economic forecasters have created genuine fear in many people, resulting in an atmosphere of unrest and anxiety. In fact, the fear of economic disaster in America has paralyzed more people than any other issue I deal with concerning emotional financial problems. So prominent is the doomsday fear in America that a society exists in Chicago called Bulletin of the Atomic Scientists. In 1947, the Bulletin established the Doomsday Clock to represent the nuclear apocalypse, and the hour it could happen. On the face of the clock is the world map. The keepers of this clock claim the threat of nuclear holocaust did not vanish with the end of the Cold War. Harry Reiser, who witnessed the first atomic blast, is quoted as saying, "We are not crying fire in the world's theater, but we do want to sound an alarm. We do want to call for increased vigilance."

Since its installation, the clock has been reset 16 times. According to the Associated Press, on December 7, 1995, the hands of the clock were moved three minutes closer to a nuclear blast — at 14 minutes before midnight.

I am not a nuclear physicist, but the invention and maintenance of a doomsday clock seems extreme.

In grade school, I can remember diving under my desk during atomic bomb drills and reading pamphlets about evacuation routes to shelters in case of a nuclear attack. Nuclear symbols on telephone poles pointed the way to basements in buildings prepared as city bomb shelters.

If it's 14 minutes to midnight, why aren't government agencies preparing and protecting us from an atomic attack as they did during the Cold War? Because today the only real threat of nuclear holocaust is in the minds of those who are paranoid about it.

**_Instead, let's look at the facts._**

That doesn't mean the world will always be safe. In some future generation a despot could come on the scene and try to conquer the world again. It has happened before, but I'm not losing any sleep over it.

The atomic scientists' paranoia over nuclear destruction reminds me of the economic doomsayers' fears about a national financial collapse. Should we wring our hands and crawl under the covers? Worry won't help, so why waste time and energy reading and maneuvering to avoid a forecasted "economic earthquake"?

## Is the Stock Market Going to Crash?

Yes — according to Peter Lynch, one of America's most renowned investment gurus. Lynch predicted the recent market crashes back in the mid-1990s.

Sooner or later it will happen. Stocks have declined 10 percent or more on 58 occasions since 1900. That's roughly one correction every two years, and on 12 of these 58 occasions, stocks have declined 25 percent or more. That's one nasty correction every six years.

The question we should be asking is: "Will we experience a crash like the one in 1929?" A look at recent history puts the answer to this question in perspective.

On October 19, 1987, the market fell more than 500 points — far more than the crash of 1929. Some stock brokers and their clients also fell out the windows.

After the 1987 crash, there was no proven adverse affect on the economy. Those who didn't panic or bail out and instead held their position fared very well during the stock market boom that followed.

The market fell again two years later on November 29, 1989. This time the correction was 180 points in one day.

On Friday, March 8, 1996, the stock market had its third-worst point drop — 171 points. This plunge, however, represented only around three percent of its value and did not even make the top 100 list of worst days for the Dow. At the end of the next trading day, Monday, March 11, the Dow showed the biggest point gain since January 17, 1991.

After the March 8 downturn, television newscasters interviewed investors and asked them how they felt about this fall in stock prices. One man answered, "I'm not worried. This is just a correction whose time had come. In fact, it's a great time to buy!"

Research analyst, Judy Meehan, points out that people have

gotten more educated since 1987. They realize this is not the end of the world and feel more comfortable investing after stocks go down.

On the other hand, Tony Spare, also a market analyst, notes that the market is becoming increasing volatile as brokers, investment banks, and specialists are less willing to step in and bid against the market, or take stocks into their inventories to counterbalance a market move. "This is a real shift from 20 or 30 years ago," Spare says.

It's true. The market was not only headed for a fall; it has fallen. Why? Because it constantly corrects itself.

Who most fears the market crashing? Those who do not invest and who know little about how the stock market works. Who fears a crash least? Those who are invested in stocks and related investment products such as equity mutual funds.

In 1975, America had 426 mutual funds worth $46 billion. In 2009, there are more than 8,000 funds worth trillions of dollars. This is a strange time.

## It Keeps Going and Going

In all the years of the ups and downs of the stock market, investors who stayed in stocks have fared better than they would have in any other investment including real estate. Since 1936, the stock market has outperformed every other investment including real estate. This has proven itself when speculators who dumped billions into the real estate market in California have now lost their fortunes.

Although billions have been lost in the markets, the recovery will be light years faster than real estate simply because, after the 2009 correction, there will not be the confidence in the real estate market there has been with the false bottom. Plus, stocks, bonds, and mutual funds are liquid, making them much more attractive in a volatile marketplace.

Sure investors get concerned when corrections are taking place, but holding onto stocks has proven to be the most prudent decision for those wishing to maintain an investment portfolio that keeps growing.

Getting a 33 percent drop in value in one day can test anyone's nerves. Taking a rise of 133 percent or more, however, in the ensuing few years following a crash can be exhilarating.

Fear of a stock market crash often leads investors to buy bonds. Bonds are almost as popular as stocks — and just as volatile. In the past 90 plus years, bonds have outperformed stocks in only one year — and that was during the 1930s. In fact, 1994 was the worst year on record for government bonds, and those of us who owned them wished we didn't.

Peter Lynch writes in his second book, *Beating the Street,* that people are living longer these days and realizing that buying bonds has left them with less money than they would need for their twilight years. Why? Because bonds provide no growth in principal.

Many financial advisors, including myself, suggest investing in stocks that pay good solid dividends. Moody's rating service of stocks shows 332 publicly traded companies had not only been paying a good dividend but also raised that dividend for 10 straight years or more. This has happened consistently in spite of the inevitable economic downturns every seven to 10 years.

When I did a study on recessionary trends from 1910 to 1995, I found that America had not only a stock market correction but also an economic correction in the form of a recession — either mild or harsh every seven to 10 years.

## The Big, Black Hole

Let's imagine a worst case scenario. Suppose the country slides into a recession that lasts for 30 years. The economy collapses, inflation makes money worthless, and the prices of goods skyrocket.

What could you have done to protect yourself from financial ruin? Nothing. If the bottom falls out, then there is nothing you can do about it.

What can you do while you are waiting for some catastrophic phenomena to happen? Stay put and make money.

Doomsayer paranoiacs don't understand that an economic disaster doesn't hit like a meteor from outer space. That could happen you know, but it isn't something most of us are losing sleep over.

A big, black hole could open up in outer space and swallow up our planet. Many variables in our universe could annihilate us. But will they? I don't know; only God knows. In the meanwhile, if I take to hiding in the cellar because I'm afraid a meteor will strike America and wipe us out, then I will miss the boat leaving for the Bahamas and a great vacation.

The same principle applies to our investment portfolio and the stock market. Trust the powers-that-be as much as you can and leave the investing up to your financial advisor. If you don't have any stocks, then don't concern yourself about the stock market crashing,

Writing in Forbes magazine, R.S. Satomon, Jr. notes:

"No meaningful correction? One of the most remarkable characteristics of this market is that it has been able to correct internally without damaging the entire market. For instance, many technology stocks are down 20 percent or more from their 1995 highs, and yet the market itself has not been hurt materially. New market leadership comes about through group rotation. This market quickly punishes companies whose earnings fall short of expectations. Just so long as excesses are corrected, there is no compelling need for the whole market to correct."

In other words, ignore the worrywarts and don't fret if you aren't taking advantage of the rising markets. The forces of supply and demand in our free market system keep the economy in checks and balances as companies compete in the marketplace.

Consider this: Without the stock market, there would be no jobs. This is far from a mute point. The stock market is where companies get money to do research and to expand.

Why am I writing about pages that have to do with the past markets? In every case when financial pressures rise and fears abound, we forget what has happened in the past when people had the same fears we have at present. The markets will rise again unless God is through evangelizing the earth through America. If that's the case, I won't be on this planet when that happens anyway.

## The Bears Are Here!

My family was on a trip one year in the Great Smoky Mountains National Park. We came face to face with our first real live bear in the wild. On a remote highway near Clingman's Dome high in the mountains of Tennessee and North Carolina, we watched in horror as a big black bear lumbered toward our car. I quickly rolled up the window.

The ferociousness and strength of that huge creature became apparent as it rose up on its hind legs and snarled at us. Like a bug, our little Volkswagen Beetle was shook, rolled on, and threatened as we clung to one another from within the safety of the car. After a few moments, the big bully sauntered away as slowly as it had appeared.

Later, we looked at one another and laughed.

Until that day, the thought of a bear attack had never bothered me. I fear bears, but I still drive through the Yosemite and Sequoia National Parks near my home, hoping to see one in their natural habitat. The fear of bears doesn't paralyze me to the point that I forego viewing the beauty of the mountains and stay away. Why? Because I know there are certain precautions I can take to keep myself from being eaten alive.

Most investors are waiting for the next bear market to come and it will — just as it has done in the past — but don't let fear of a bear market paralyze you and keep you from the investment opportunities that are always available. Too many people have missed reaping profits because paranoia forced them to take up residence in the bomb shelter.

Take precautions, keep tabs on your investments, get sound advice, and refuse to listen to the fear mongers. They want you to be as miserable as they are.

As for me, I am as afraid of an explosive unrecoverable market crash as I am of a huge grizzly storming into my house and devouring the contents of the refrigerator — and you should be as well.

## Volatile World Markets?

Talking about "world markets" is like talking about God. No one has ever seen Him, fewer people are going to church these days to learn about Him, but when you mention His name, suddenly everybody is an expert.

Ignorance bred by fear always creates contusion. No wise investor will confine himself to our national market. Why? Because 40 percent of the registered companies on the New York Stock Exchange are domiciled offshore. Investments in the world market must be a portion of any portfolio.

When I was studying for my MBA in International Business, I

learned that world markets will crash, and they do all the time. The Japanese stock market has had 15 corrections in the last 10 years. Some of these have been very severe; yet the Japanese market rebounds and remains a strong force in the world's economy.

For years the doomsayers have been telling us that the fall of the Japanese markets would cause a crash in the American stock markets. This has been proven false over and over again. In fact, every crash of the Japanese stock market has opened up opportunities for American investors as stocks crept downward. The Japanese markets and the American markets are not interrelated; they are competitive, and the pressure of the Japanese markets means zero to the Americans.

During the last crash, the Japanese market fell drastically. On that same day, and the days following, the New York Stock Exchange remained very strong and even hit a record high.

Emerging markets rise and fall. Who can forget when Argentina had hyperinflation and a runaway economy? One of the most risky places on the globe to invest was in Argentina. Even though their economy collapsed three times since 1975 (most recently in 2002), they recovered; so our problems cannot be equated to that economy. Ten thousand percent inflation will not happen in America, nor can it.

At the writing of this book, Mexico's peso has collapsed, and no immediate nations are coming forward to bail them out. The corruption in Mexico makes it an unstable place to invest. However, this was not always true.

Investors have made a flood of money pouring money into Telephones De Mexico (Mexican telephone company), one of the strongest stocks on the NYSE. Cifra, which is the Mexican Wal-Mart and the largest retailer in Mexico, turned out to be a great growth stock.

When Cifra was considered a risky stock, I bought it at 85 cents per share and then sold it a few months later at $3.20 per share. Not a bad return for a stock from an underprivileged country. That company is now Wal-Mart de Mexico, and the stock shares that belonged to the owners of Cifra are happy.

In the last few years, other good investments have been made south of the border. Mexico will stabilize at some point in time, and then more bargains will be found.

Investors have also made a lot of money in the Tiger Funds of the Pacific Rim nations — Singapore, Taiwan, Korea, and especially Hong Kong. In 1997, however, Britain turned Hong Kong over to the Chinese, making investing there questionable.

While doing research for a dissertation on *How the Hong Kong Treaty of 1997 Will Affect the Economy in the Philippines and Related Countries,* I learned a lot about this treaty. But one question remains unanswered: Why did the British agree to let Hong Kong revert back to the Chinese? My lack of understanding in this matter, and because I don't trust the Chinese communists at this point, makes me doubt the wisdom of investing any money in that part of the world.

## Competing in the Open Market

Investing in the governments of other countries is far different from investing in companies whose headquarters are in those countries. Companies of the world compete in the open marketplace. This vast system lends itself to good profit sharing providing you choose the right company in which to invest. Of course, that is true no matter what the investment.

When thinking about world markets, consider the stability of the country where the industry resides. I would be leery of investing in a company domiciled in any African nation except South Africa. The instability of these governments directly affects the way a company is permitted to operate, the taxes involved, and who actually runs the business.

The opposite is true of European nations, where the governments are relatively stable. Some of the world's greatest companies are headquartered in Europe. However, you must be careful about investing in the currencies and bonds of these countries. The ongoing, heated debate about unifying the European currencies causes the markets there to be very volatile.

In 1992, most of the European countries ratified the Maastricht Treaty, which laid out the criteria that each nation must meet in order for the currency to be unified. As of November 1995, only Luxembourg, Germany, and Ireland had met the criteria. In fact, no other nations, except Denmark, were in striking distance of making the grade, according to Steven H. Hanke's Forbes article, *Turmoil in*

*Europe,* for the November 20, 1995 issue. Today, 15 of 27 European countries are unified with the Euro.

Although Germany had to finance the restructuring of their nation after the Berlin Wall fell in 1989, it is by far the strongest still of the G-7 countries. In fact, the Germans have one of the most powerful economies in the world.

Much of what happens in America depends in part on what the strong Bundesbank does with the German Mark against the U.S. dollar. The European currencies are mostly unified but not without a price. The Germans have had to give up their powerful Mark for a sure weaker, unified European currency. The stumbling block the Germans suspected that the French will try to do in Bundesbank if the currencies ratified is very real.

All of this turmoil has taken its toll on the German Mark. Germany has dumped billions of dollars in cash into banks in Switzerland — another very strong economy. Normally, the German bond market outperforms the U.S. markets, but because of the nervousness of the Germans the opposite is true. The German markets are under the U.S. markets for a rare time.

What does all this mean to the potential investor? A weak unified European currency would be no substitute for the Deutsche Mark.

Be careful about investing in European currencies, including the Mark, but feel free to invest in their strong companies which the governments of these nations protect on the open market.

Keep in mind that the world markets will do what they have done since Marco Polo went to Asia and discovered silks and magic carpets. There will always be commerce between the nations because of the products that are made and the need for the countries to sell them. Politics at times, however, makes trading volatile but not impossible.

## Is Opportunity Knocking?

How does it look on the global scene? I believe we are decades away from having to worry about any kind of worldwide collapse. Why?

One reason is the rapid development of the third world nations. These countries are opening up new markets. The Four Tigers —

Singapore, Hong Kong, Taiwan, Korea — are giving the Japanese competition.

Harry Dent, in his book, *The Great Boom Ahead,* states that these fiercely competitive nations have indeed become second, not third world countries in the 1980s. An example is Korea, which has moved its automobile line into the United States and other countries all over the world.

China's tremendous economic potential lies in its huge population, caches of untapped natural resources, and vast land of diversified peoples. The Chinese have already made agreements with international companies to open manufacturing plants that will put their populace to work and move their nation far into the 21st century.

> ***Opportunity is knocking - not disaster.***

True, it will take decades for this to happen, but while it is happening, the world marketplace will receive a lot of positive input.

What will keep the world marketplace in sync with the strong growth the United States will be experiencing during this time? The emergence of the middle class in these third world nations. Opportunity is knocking – not disaster.

Communism is dead except in North Korea and Cuba. The fall of communist regimes has opened up the Eastern bloc of countries to world trade. These nations want free trade, and the trend is toward a democratic form of government all over the world.

Elections are being held in nations that never before dreamed of having a voice in their leadership. Corruption abounds, however, and the critics focus on this unfortunate aspect of freedom. But, the opportunity exists like never before. Once these nations function as democracies, the taste of freedom will never leave them. Freedom creates opportunity, and opportunity in these countries spells new markets for products "made in the USA."

What about polarization between third-world nations? Most third world countries are free to trade their raw materials (things they cannot manufacture) and trade their commodities.

Sony produced a video at a conference they hosted which was

an eye opener about the time we live in. Although the video was produced in 2008, the video shows and tells what will drive the economy. Just these changes in the markets will boggle the mind.

- 25% of India's highest IQs out number the entire population of the United States.
- The top 10 jobs in demand in 2010 did not exist in 2004.
- We are now educating students for jobs that don't exist and to use technologies that haven't been invented. Yet, one-half of what students are learning now will be outdated in four years.

We are living in exponential times, and this is one reason why those people who have lost their homes and jobs are feeling there will never be an end to the madness, but there will be.

So many things are present that will create opportunities and drive the economy. Read some of the old commentary by news reporters, writers, and even some economists during the last deep recession, lasting from 1980 to 1982. Nothing that is happening now would have been possible according to them. Here is a synopsis from Sony's Video that illustrates how graphic this statement really is:

The number of text messages sent each day exceeds the entire population of the planet. The first text message was sent in 1992. This is absolutely amazing since we have been so accustomed to texting that we feel it has been around for a lifetime. Nor did we have telephones saturated throughout America 100 years ago.

How fast has the Internet changed our world? It took radio 38 years to reach an audience of 50 million people. Television was 23 years reaching this milestone. In contrast, the Internet only took four years to accomplish what its cousins took years to do. Apple iPods took three years; Facebook took two.

In 1984, the Internet was in its infancy and had 1,000 users. In 1992, there were 1,000,000 (one million) subscribers. In 2008, 1,000,000,000 (one billion) people are logged on to the Internet.

The Internet will drive the world, and the super age of communication will create multitudes of employment and invention opportunities for the entire population. The Internet will drive the third world countries to that middle class more than progressive economists and advisers have predicted since it exploded on the scene.

## A New World Order?

In 1990, when President George H. Bush commented during a speech to Congress about a "New World Order," religionists feared the United States was about to embark into some New Age Revolution that would align us with the Antichrist. The "new world" President Bush was referring to has to do with the reorganization of governments because of the crash of communism.

The world is reorganizing itself for the future and for the better. While the incredible technological advances of the past 75 years have made life in the United States, Canada, and Europe freer, cleaner, and more pleasurable, the same hasn't been true in other areas of the globe. In fact, primitive cultures still exist, and even some civilized nations are still years away from modernization. This is all changing now and will continue to change in the near future.

On a trip to Europe a few years ago, I was astounded by the difference between the Western world and the Eastern bloc countries. After boarding a train in Austria, my companions and I headed toward Budapest, Hungary. As we approached the Hungarian border, I noticed the many well-groomed farms on the Austrian side. In fact, one farmer was plowing his field in an air conditioned tractor as he listened to music on his head set.

When the train crossed to the Hungarian side of the border, however, farmers were working the same fertile ground where the same rain fell on similar soil and the same sunshine gave warmth to the seeds and crops in the ground. But the Hungarians were toiling the ground with oxen while nearby an old tractor sat rusting in the field.

This depressing picture will soon change for Hungary and the other poor European nations. Opportunities will be created by the United States as we take advantage of the economic needs of these freedom-loving Eastern third world countries.

## The Hungry Giant

Malcolm Forbes said, "China's on a roll, and if Deng's vital organs hang in there for two or three more years, no reactionary Red ideologues will be able to stamp out China's entrepreneurial prairie fires. By permitting free marketing of production that exceeds quotas in agriculture, manufacturing, and services, Deng has ignited that slumbering, massive Chinese potential."

Andrew Tanzer, in his Forbes article, "China's Ravenous Appetite" wrote: "What are the three things driving global agriculture today? China, China, China. That country's going to continue to be a tremendous influence on agricultural commodities over the next five or ten years. You're dealing with gigantic population needs; so gigantic that it's a bit scary." Tanzer was quoting Bruce Scherr, a commodities research expert and the chief operating officer of Sparks Companies, a food research firm in Memphis, Tennessee.

The Chinese are already moving away from their mundane diet of rice, beans, and cabbage they have endured for years under communist rule. Today they are eating more fish, eggs, and meat.

Why focus on China? Because China is huge! China grows at a population rate, according to Tanzer, of 14 million people a year and makes up 21 percent of the world's total population. At the same time, China has only a small portion of agricultural land compared to their huge population.

As changes in the Chinese diet persist, the 12 million tons of wheat they are now importing will only rise. Also, they are beginning to eat more beef, which will put bigger and bigger demands on the Western world for supply. As the beef needs escalate, this will force the Chinese to grow more corn to feed the cattle. China already had increased their imports of corn from 105 million tons (1995) by late 2005. This cavernous appetite will continue to grow as the food chain becomes more sophisticated.

## Egg Rolls and Big Macs

I have eaten at some of the largest McDonalds restaurants in the world, and they happen to be in China. The Chinese — who love fast food — also enjoy chicken. As a result, Kentucky Fried Chicken franchises are booming in China's cities. Still only the slightest dent has been made in the overwhelming potential for fast-food restaurants in China.

The Chinese must drink something with their Big Macs, right? You can bet Coca Cola and Pepsi, who have been on the scene for many years, are continuing to gear up as the foreign beer companies are doing. Even some Chinese soft drinks are pretty good.

As Chinese youth move from the hillsides to the cities, the demand for products from nearly every producing country of the world will increase — and with it their economies as they scamper to compete in the world markets for Chinese trade.

As the Chinese are moving quickly from the 19th century into the 21st century, new world markets are being created. China will become the number one English-speaking country in the world.

What nation will benefit the most from the awakening of the Chinese political, economic, and social system? The United States. Why? Because we are the inventors and producers of most of what the Chinese people want. They are rapidly shedding the traditional Mao Tse Tung dull robes for Levi's and exchanging their sandals for Asics and Nikes.

At the same time that China is opening up to foreign investors, budding Chinese entrepreneurs are also prospering. The Liu brothers of the Chinese Hope Group pawned their watches, bicycles, and other belongings to raise $500 capital, so they could start raising pigs, quail, chickens, and ducks.

Why? Because they realized the Chinese were eating more meat, which is a status symbol in China. Liu Yonghao says "When people have more money, the first thing they'll spend it on is food."

Starting with a meager investment, the Liu brothers have now amassed enough money to be founding shareholders of the first private bank allowed in China since the early 1950s. Liu says, "I feel blessed because I grew up during a period when China moved from a planned economy to a market economy. There hasn't been an opportunity like this in China in 100 years."

Other third world countries offer the same market potential. As the people of these countries demand access to the products and foods of other nations, the world will become America's marketplace.

## America's Future in a Global Market

Former Russian states that have broken off from Moscow rule will not align themselves with the powerful Germans and for good reason. Afraid of German domination, these newly formed independent countries do not trust the Germans, whose thirst for power and influence goes all the way back to Huns and Goths of centuries ago.

The Germans enjoy a position of tremendous influence, affluence, and domination, but only to a degree in Western Europe. Any movement economically will trigger a response from Germany to be in the middle of new developments.

All of this repositioning of the Eastern European nations creates business opportunities for the United States on the horizon.

Richard Nixon once questioned, "Are we going to be asking who lost Russia?"

Harry Dent, in his book, *The Great Boom Ahead,* writes, "We must make it a high priority to establish our economic interests in Eastern Europe. Otherwise, economic dominance there is going to eventually go overwhelmingly to Europe, and we're going to be locked out of one of the major growth areas and important consumer markets in the New World Economic Order."

I couldn't agree more. The United States already maintains a strong place of leadership in the world markets.

Not long ago, someone commented to me, "The dollar is taking one of its repetitious daily plunges in the world currency markets. Eventually America's weak dollar will be so impotent that it will collapse against more powerful currencies."

Rather than go into a long explanation about the strengths and weaknesses of the dollar and the causes of the dollar rising and falling, I used this illustration: "Sir," I said, "I challenge you to go to any country in the world and pull out a dollar and try to pay for something with it. You will then find out just how respected and strong the dollar is."

That example represents the outstanding position of our country — a position that is weakening today because of recession, but will rebound when the economy strengthens, which it will.

Many philosophers and evangelicals of today are afraid of this progress because they think it spells the end of the world. The alliances that nations make with each other will always be a threat that the end is near.

## But Let's Be Realistic

As global competition heats up, huge corporations will be aligning with these newly free countries and taking advantage of their work forces. As a result, nations will be implementing technological training, resulting in the exchange of manufacturing, industrial, and business trade information between these countries and corporations.

The companies themselves will implement and underwrite much of the cost for this education because it serves their interests. Corporations will move into these nations and put the people to work. This creates greater personal income and, at the same time, new buyers for American goods — but only if the U.S. is in the position to take advantage of the situation.

On the other hand, is another powerful nation liable to emerge in the distant future? That is anybody's guess, but I don't think so — at least not in our lifetimes. History repeats itself.

The world scene in the future, depending upon what the United States does, is set for another powerful nation — like the United States — to rise up. Let's hope it is a Christian nation founded on democracy and freedom.

I have no fear of a worldwide famine, or a worldwide depression. I have more fear of the world leaders blowing themselves up with dynamite than I do with money.

## Doomsday Economics

On what do those who predict the demise of the American economy base their theories? By trying to prove that runaway inflation or hyperinflation will destroy us. Read any of the doomsayer books, and you will find a prediction concerning hyperinflation.

As far back as the early 1980s, religious financial consultant Larry Burkett was telling his followers — and continued to tell until his untimely death in 2003 — that "one day the nation will experience the ravages of hyperinflation."

In the bestseller doomsday book, *Bankruptcy 1995,* Harry Figgie says "Unless the people's government in Washington, D.C., makes drastic changes in its fiscal policies now, the typical American family will be fortunate in 1995 if it can feed and house itself, and even then not in the manner to which it has become accustomed."

Well, 1995 has come and gone, and most typical Americans are warm and cozy, eating well, and even prospering in many cases during a deep recession that Figgie and others predicted would be our demise.

Figgie goes on to say, "While we can't be certain exactly how the tragedy of America's economic collapse will unfold, we can be pretty certain that the bottom will drop out of the American economy in either one of two ways or in some combination of both. Probably we'll get a taste of both hyperinflation and panic. Hyperinflation or market panic or any combination will finish off America and Americans."

I could provide other examples because the Internet is inundated by those who are preaching once again we have hit an iceberg and are sinking like the Titanic. The attitude of these prophets of gloom remains essentially the same. In order for these theories to have validity, certain irreversible economic variables must be in place. These are:

### 1. Out-of-control spending by consumers.

According to the proponents of the hyperinflation theory, a sure sign the economy is super inflating is proven by the buying habits of the public. The public fuels inflation by spending. This can only happen if inflation is rising because this creates uncontrollable spending habits in the consumers. As the consumer sees prices decline, he is motivated to spend before prices begin to rise. This adds production to the already serious problem.

According to Burkett, "Young couples see their dream homes slipping away, so they extend beyond what normally would be prudent to buy that home. Investors see their paper assets eroding, so they rush out to buy real assets such as land, buildings, precious metals, and the like."

Larry Burkett was right. Today, that is exactly what has happened. The quest for larger homes fueled by a bottomless lending market has created the record number of foreclosures in 2009 – and beyond. The above reference was written in the early 1990s when Burkett believed an economic earthquake would happen then because of the debt. This happened before from 1979-1982 when it seemed the whole world was in foreclosure. We rebounded then, and we will rebound again. Young couples will buy their first home, people will trade up in value, and the American dream will be alive and well.

### 2. Consumer debt.

The fearsome — who don't believe in debt of any kind — think Americans are squandering their equities and will have nothing left.

As a result, federal and state governments won't be able to pay their debts, and America as we know it will come to a screeching halt.

### 3. The government keeps printing money, adding to the problem.

If the government keeps this up, according to the doomsayers, the middle class will be wiped out, and those living on fixed incomes will be impoverished. Examples such as Argentina, Chile, Brazil, and Mexico are used to prove that when the government prints money, it automatically leads to hyperinflation and economic collapse.

What is hyperinflation? Simply put, it occurs when a country loses confidence in its currency. There is a vast difference, however, between the economies of Latin and South American countries and the United States. Not once in the history of the United States has hyperinflation been a problem — or ever going to be a problem. Why? Because our economy has always been strong.

In many countries where hyperinflation has destroyed their economies, the government owns the businesses or is in partnership with the business owners. That is not true in the United States.

Our government encourages free enterprise. Free enterprise promotes entrepreneurship. Entrepreneurship promotes competition. Competition keeps prices in check.

When necessary our government does print money, but the reasons are vastly different from those of hyper-inflated economies. The United States has learned how to control inflation either by shrinking the supply or by putting more money into the economy. Hyper-inflated economies print money to inflate their currency to keep it from collapsing. The opposite occurs, of course, and the currency collapses anyway.

## Inflation - On Our Side

One afternoon, during a Pittsburgh radio talk show, I debated a congressman from California. Although very conservative and someone I support, he believes in the economic calamities generally accepted by pessimistic doomsayer writers.

The host of the program asked, "Do you think the United States should be on a gold standard?"

"Absolutely," the congressman replied. "We need to fix our currency to that standard."

Fixing our currency to a commodity such as gold has been and still is the subject of hot debate. The congressman tried to prove that because of gold's intrinsic value.

Gold does have intrinsic value, which means you can break a bar of gold into certain parts and one part has the same value in proportion as the entire bar. One ounce of gold has 1/16th value of a pound, which never depreciates even if the bar is broken into pieces, like diamonds or other precious stones would be. This does not mean, however, that our currency needs to be fixed to a gold standard.

When the talk show host asked whether or not I believed we should be on the gold standard, my reply was "Absolutely not."

The host then asked me, "Why aren't we on the gold standard today?"

"We are not on the gold standard for the same reason we went off the gold standard in 1971. We can't control inflation by being fixed to a commodity," I replied.

I was then able to ask the good congressman to explain what would have happened to the U.S. economy after the October 1987 stock market crash if we had been fixed to the gold standard. When I received no intelligible reply, I answered the question myself.

"If we had been fixed to the gold standard," I explained, "we would have gone stone-cold bankrupt. The Federal Reserve would not have been able to inflate the economy permanently, or temporarily, while fixed to gold. Instead, the action taken by the Feds in 1987 proved to be one of their most prudent. What did they do? They pumped the economy full of money."

So judicious was this action that three months after the stock market crash, there was no proven adverse effect on the economy. In fact, little more than six months after the crash, you would barely have known it happened. Americans have learned to control our economy through this sophisticated and complicated bartering system called "fiat money" that we have figured out how to make work.

## I Predict!

I predicted that before the end of the 1990s and before the

beginning of a new century, the United States was going to see some remarkable changes in its economy. Why? Because of new leadership and renewed strength in the country's future as it deals with the 21st century.

In 1990, on a videotaped lecture called "The End of the Cold War and Its Effect on the Economy in the 1990s," I predicted the Dow Jones Industrial Average (DJIA) would reach 5,000 by mid 1996. I missed that prediction. The DJIA hit 5,000 in mid 1995, coming sooner than I expected!

I then went out on a limb while writing an investment book and predicted the market would reach 10,000 by the year 2000. I missed that mark by two years. The market hit 10,000 in 1998. The doomsayers said the market would have completely crashed, and the nation would be broke.

How could I make such bold predictions? Because of low inflation, which by the way we still have; so here I go with another prediction. I predict the market will rise to 15,000 by 2012 and upwards from there as the economy rebounds.

For many years, the pessimistic economists have been predicting that inflation will be rampant, but the opposite has been true. Ask anyone who owns a house in California about falling inflation rates and the effect on the real estate market.

I believe the dollar will strengthen as much as 15 percent from its present level. To what can this be attributed? To the low inflation rate.

For one decade, from 1985 to 1995, the dollar was in decline. The dollar is in decline today, but there is nothing concrete to keep the dollar weak in the marketplace for any sustainable period of time.

American businesses are number one on the world markets in competition, and that trend will continue as the country's economy gets stronger. The stock market will take a positive view of this change in the dollar's strength and fortify itself as well.

## A Rising Dollar

What will a rising dollar do for the economy? There are several things that will benefit all Americans:

**1. The trade deficit shrinks as the price on imports reduces.**

As a result, other countries will be able to afford our products, thus spurring economic growth.

**2. Traders invest in dollars, which causes the overall improvement of economic conditions.**

The stronger the dollar, the more our currency is purchased on the world market.

**3. The rising strength of the dollar has a positive effect on interest rates.**

How? Rates begin to fall. In mid–1995, interest rates in the United States were higher than many European countries, including Germany, Switzerland and Asiatic countries, such as Japan. Today, they are the lowest in decades.

**4. Interest rates fall when the currency strengthens and investors realize this is not a temporary situation.**

Market statistics have proved this true time and again.

**5. As the dollar falls, the Consumer Confidence Index will rise, giving the economy a boost.**

Why? Because private investors will pour more money from savings into American business investments. The Consumer Confidence Indicator, which measures how American businesses feel about present conditions, is one of the indexes used to determine the nation's economic strength.

John Dessauer, a writer for HealthWealth magazine, says the dollar will rise by 20 percent but there is danger of a correction. "The coming surge in confidence could spark a massive wave of buying U.S. stocks," notes Dessauer. "The U.S. stock market could rise so high that we have no choice but to sell."

A great sell off would cause the market to correct itself, creating many losers among investors who were not diversified enough in their investment portfolios. The next go round should show the awareness investors have as they have learned from their own mistakes. Many will miss opportunities because the losses overwhelmed them, and they won't take any more risks.

Dessauer also cautions about another negative condition that can arise from growth that is too fast: "I worry that the dollar won't just recover by 20 percent but will continue to rise until it poses a real threat to U.S. corporations." This was a 1997 prediction, but it has validity, and many people reading this chapter late in 2010 will see the parallels.

I agree with caution, but let's take our chances with positive growth and the negative effect it would have on the stock market versus the mentality of the Feds in the last 20 years — a philosophy that has taken away many opportunities for America to break from stagnation by keeping the economy much too cool.

## A Bright Future Ahead

After reading all the ensuing problems concerning inflation, has it been a real threat to us?

Today, in the first decade of the 21st Century and the second Millennium, nothing the doomsayers have predicted will come to pass. Why? Because inflation is not a problem in America. In fact, the rate of inflation is the lowest it has been for 34 years and will probably stay that way for a long time. Low inflation rates increase the chances of a stable economy for years to come.

If, indeed, spending habits and consumer debt are created by inflation, then we are in pretty good shape. Consumer spending is up while consumer debt is declining. Americans are saving more than at any time in our nation's history.

Consumer equilibrium is the balance between consumption and savings. Although some American families are in trouble and highly stressed, most American families function very well and are saving money through their profit sharing and other forms of Investment Retirement Accounts.

Fear of the stock market crashing, anxiety that the world economy will fall apart, apprehension that money will lose its value and leave us all destitute — these are very real concerns. We can't just stick our heads in the sand like the ostrich and hope everything turns out all right.

If, however, we don't pay strict attention to the politics of these factors, then we could fall back into pre-1994 days. For 40 years, the liberal schizophrenics ruled our government, creating most of our economic problems and generating financial paranoia throughout the nation. They have re-seized control of Congress and are at it again.

The great economist, Adam Smith, summed up the problem of

fear and its effect on the economy better than anyone I have ever heard or read:

*"Can it all come tumbling down? In a paper market, based on belief, this fear is universal, no matter how deeply it is buried. Sure, it can all come tumbling down. All it takes is for belief to go away. Fear is no help to functioning in the marketplace, as some of the senior generation can tell you, so it doesn't do to walk around with it every day. Most of the investment world, blazing its way through the trees has little idea of the forest. We all live by a thread anyway, so it may make no more sense to worry about financial H-bombs than plutonium ones."*

By believing and feeding upon the negative all the time, we could destroy ourselves. But by faith and hard work, we can keep this country growing to greater and greater heights. I have all the faith in the world everything will be just fine.

## CHAPTER TEN

# AMERICA: STILL THE LAND OF OPPORTUNITY

Is the economy going to go bust around the year 2010? If not, what can you do to ensure your future?

Let me make it clear from the outset that I do not believe the American economy is headed for bankruptcy. I do not believe a depression is imminent now or at any time in the near future. Doomsayers have been saying this for years, but 99.9 percent of what they predict never comes true and instead the opposite happens. What little does happen that drives us to hide under rocks and old boards is so insignificant it barely needs mentioning.

If a well-known doomsayer tells you the stock market is going broke in the next few months, I suggest you go out and buy all the stocks you can. Why? Because more than likely the market will be setting new records just like it has done for all the years after a recession. Then, while the paranoids are sitting on their nest eggs, you'll be making money.

Suppose it is 1979, and some seer tells you that in the next decade, several terrible events are going to take place:

- American hostages will be captured by a Persian Government and held for 256 days, and the United States will not be able to get them out.

- The President will be shot and wounded by a would-be assassin.
- Interest rates will climb to 22 percent as measured by the prime rate.
- Home mortgages will be as high as 15 percent, making it nearly impossible for mainstream America to qualify for a home loan.
- Banks and Savings and Loans will go broke in record numbers.
- The Federal Savings and Loan Insurance Corporation (FSLIC) will go out of business.
- The unemployment rate will reach 10.6 percent.
- The stock market will crash falling over 500 points in one day and fall greater than the Great Depression of 1929.

In light of such events, what would you have done with your money? How much pressure would there have been to bury your money as far underground as you could get it? All these events did happen in the 1980s; but if you stuck your head in the sand, you missed the greatest economic boom in American history.

## Underground? or Off the Wall?

The same doomsayers who predicted the demise of America in the 1980s are still around today.

What were they saying back then? Popular religious perpetrators of bad news still have daily radio programs and are writing books that are filled with horrific predictions.

The following excerpts deal with Mr. Larry Burkett's predictions, who is no longer living. He and I disagreed from opposite sides of the fence for years, so I have no intention except to show that even the most prominent Christian financial people should stay with practical, every day advice and run away from predictions concerning the economy when they are ill-equipped and inexperienced to do so. He wrote the book I'm quoting, not me, so I am only trying to illustrate how far off-the-wall doomsayers will go to make their point; even good Christian men with good moral intentions.

In Larry Burkett's book, *How to Prosper in the Underground Economy,* written in 1982, Burkett tried to prove that the 1980s would be an economic fiasco complete with stock market crashes, currency collapse, runaway inflation upward of 20 percent, unemployment over 15 percent, and takeovers by gangs raiding your homes.

What was Burkett's advice in light of these ominous predictions? "Take your children into the wilderness with no provisions for a week and teach them to forage for food." As a solution to the economic collapse, he unsuccessfully tried to intertwine a bartering system and other such nonsense.

His investment advice is even more shocking — which seems ironic since he predicted the total collapse of the economy in the 1980s and, to my knowledge, never ran an investment portfolio of any kind in any public manner. In Chapter 12, *The Complete Underground Investment Portfolio,* Burkett writes, "I don't encourage my clients to get involved with mutual funds because in general they have had poor growth records."

Concerning common stocks he advises, "Common stocks are a very poor growth investment for the vast majority of investors."

His advice concerning real estate, if followed, must have set back a lot of people:

"Apartment and office buildings will be an excellent growth investment during the 1980s. Building and financing costs will continue to escalate so rapidly that the sooner individuals can get into one of these investments, the more opportunity they'll have to experience significant appreciation. The best way to get into big buildings with a moderate amount of money is to join a limited partnership, which will enable you to pool your money with other small or medium-sized investors. As a limited partner, you limit your losses to the amount of money you've put up."

On page 210, Burkett recommends oil and gas exploration. Why? "Because I believe the price of both oil and gas has to go up significantly in the next five years. Also, they represent a real, tangible investment which should make it safely through any currency crisis."

In this case, ignorance is not bliss — it is dangerous. Keep in mind that there are a lot of would-be financial experts running around who aren't financial experts at all. Their advice should be taken with a grain of salt.

Was Mr. Burkett's advice accurate back in 1982? Apparently not. The stock market has outperformed all other forms of investments, including real estate, since 1936. In the early part of this decade, new records were set almost every week in the stock market and investment accounts swelled.

What if we had ignored Mr. Burkett's advice in 1982 and instead of not investing in mutual funds put $10,000 into John Templeton's Foreign Fund and left it alone? By 2,000 the investment would have been worth $1 million!

What about Burkett's prediction of runaway inflation up to 20 percent? It never happened. Instead, inflation in the 1980s fell to around 3.5 percent. Unemployment was the lowest in decades, the stock market boomed, and not one gang raided my pantry!

Ask the people in Houston, Texas, about oil and gas leasing projects. I am sure Mr. Burkett's clients lost a lot of money in the 1980s.

How about real estate? Prudential-Bache (now Prudential Securities) had to pay back hundreds of millions of dollars because of a class action suit won against them in court. Why? For losing millions of dollars to their investors in real estate limited partnerships involving — guess what — big apartment projects.

Why did I select excerpts from Larry Burkett's book? To illustrate how improper advice creates downward pressure on ordinary people who then make bad financial decisions.

The same doomsayers making idiotic statements today are the ones who predicted that the now corrected and depressed stock market would crash and burn a long time ago, and even though it is down in the throes of this recession, it is far from demise.

## The Best Advice

Being afraid all the time is not the way to live. Instead, keep abreast of current events at all times. Don't depend on one person as the source of all your information. As you educate yourself on the issues, you will be able to make sound financial decisions.

The best advice I can give is, "Invest and let go." If anything of great apocalyptic proportions occurs, then money wouldn't be worth anything anyway. Besides, what could you do to safeguard your finances against a total economic collapse that would affect not only your own demise but that of everyone else?

During the Cold War with the Soviet Union in the late 50s, our neighbors built a bomb shelter. About that same time, someone wrote a letter to "Dear Abby" asking if she intended to or had built a bomb shelter.

Abigail Van Buren's reply was classic, and probably the same advice I would give someone trying to escape a cashless, worthless monetary system. Dear Abby replied this way: "We have chosen not to build a bomb shelter. Why would we want to be alive two weeks after everyone else is dead?"

Taking extreme precautions with your money and hedging against a future economic chaos is senseless. Chances are it will never happen in the way the preachers of doom predict. And if it were to happen at some point in your lifetime, there would be absolutely nothing you could do with any fortune you may have saved anyway. The government would take it, or some extenuating circumstance would render whatever nest egg you had worthless.

On the other hand, suppose economic conditions remain status quo into the present millennium? If you jump ship now, you will miss great investment opportunities.

## A Great Boom Ahead?

Is the economy going to go belly up? I don't think so. Instead, I believe a great boom towards the end of 2010 will begin and will extend well into the next couple of decades.

Harry S. Dent, Jr., author of *The Great Boom Ahead,* invented the "Generation Wave Theory." At the outset of his book, Dent writes, "Get ready for an unprecedented economic boom. Forget what some experts are saying about a slow, measured growth of the economy. Forget what the doomsayers are saying about a depression."

His theory is based upon research going back 3,000 years, which shows what happens economically after a population boom occurs about every 500 years or so. This theory proves that about 40 to 50 years after a population explosion — like the baby boom after World War II — when these babies have reached age 50, they will have evolved into an incredible power structure.

The baby boomers born in 1946 are the largest single-age population on the earth and are coming to the peak of their purchasing and spending power. This large generation born after World War II —

from 1946 to 1962 — has created ever-increasing demands that must be met. The boomers have made their money, saved their money, and in the late years of their lives will be spending it. This will help create the boom for the next few generations. As a result, creative people will develop fresh innovations to meet the aging boomers' demand for new products and commodities.

That's why I am very optimistic about the coming years. In fact, it may be one of the greatest periods in history. This is not the time to head for the hills or build a bomb shelter. To waste all your resources in an effort to avoid disaster would be a terrible blunder.

In the next few years, there will be more Bill Gates of Microsoft fame, along with hundreds and hundreds of other baby-boomer billionaires. The American dream is not lost — it is just beginning. As more and more demands are made worldwide, business expansion is inevitable.

On what do I base my optimism? Let me give you a few reasons why I believe we are going to see a boom in the future — and not a bust.

### 1. Oil prices will continue to drop.

Doomsayers are always predicting that oil prices are going to rise. Back in the 80s, this was the big concern. Would oil rise, or would oil fall?

Beginning in the fall of 2007 and continuing into the fall of 2008, oil prices hit unprecedented historical highs. It looked like the end of the world. The economy nose-dived based on the energy of those rising prices. The SUV truck market sunk like an anchor, which it probably should since Americans live like there is no tomorrow.

"Why did you buy that green car?" my friend asked, not referring to the color of the sedan, but to the fact it is a Toyota Prius.

"I'm sticking it to the man," I replied.

I was careful to explain that the purchase of this well-designed hybrid automobile was a statement rather than an attempt to save money – although that entered into the equation. I wanted to be part of that generation who is fed up with OPEC, and the Arab Nations bleeding America, and most of the world, dry.

Gas prices went through the roof, or at least as far as America is concerned. The doomsayers frothed at the mouth and tore at their hair positive that the end was finally here they had gleefully anticipated for decades.

What happened? Oil prices have fallen.

Before the present decade is over, the price of oil may fall near 1970 prices. Cheaper oil means fuel for cars and homes will be less expensive. Less money going out means more money for potential savings — at least for those who have the discipline to put money aside for the future.

*Foreign oil suppliers fear the invention and intervention of new technology.*

New energy technology comes on the scene almost every day. When I was growing up, most people heated their homes with coal or wood. The environment was polluted, and people feared the loss of our forests because of the demand in part for fuel. Today natural gas has become a major source of energy that is cleaner and cost effective. New electric furnaces and heat pumps efficiently heat and cool homes and office buildings.

I built a large home on a farm. I heated and cooled the entire house with a Geothermal System that was so cost effective that heating and cooling were way down the list on priorities to budget.

In the near future, innovative energy sources will be introduced to save the amount of oil used to make gasoline for transportation. The technology to produce electric automobiles and trains is presently being fine-tuned and will soon be available to the public. California already has a law requiring that 10 percent of the cars on the road must be electric by year 2005. We've missed this deadline and another is sure to come, but it won't matter – electric cars, hybrids, hydrogen will be upon us very soon.

Investment advisors are predicting that American automobile stocks will rise exponentially as the big three are going at lightning speed to replace the combustion engine, which surely will come to pass.

What will be the result of this competition from alternate energy sources? The price of oil will continue to drop for decades as the Persian Gulf countries try to keep ahead and slow the development

---
**I will miss the combustion engine.**
---

of technological advances. They have had a blank check for too long and will watch their fortunes disappear like the smoke from their oil pots.

## 2. Fallen mortgage rates will stabilize for a long period of time.

The trend toward lower interest rates is already underway. Some economists predict home mortgages will drop farther by the end of the decade, and this time it won't be Adjustable Rate Mortgages (ARMs) that are time bombs going off some time in the future. People will actually be able to purchase long-term mortgages at rates that were popular in the 1950s.

What will the economic ramifications be? A boom in the largest industry in the world — the construction business. With lower rates, more people can qualify for a home mortgage, creating an explosion in the home-buying market for years to come.

## 3. Inflation will be nearly stagnant for two or three decades.

During the early 1990s, the home buying market suffered, and many people lost equity in their homes. Why did this happen? Because the prices of homes in most areas of the country had skyrocketed during the previous 30 years. Once the initial shock of lower prices wears off, however, homes will become more affordable.

In decades past, inflation drove the prices of homes upward. Today, inflation is low and not expected to increase. As a result, the home market will stabilize. People will once again purchase homes — not as a high-yield investment as it was during the 1960s, '70s, and '80s — but for their practicality.

In most situations, low inflation means a stagnant economy — but that will not be the case as we near the end of the first decade of the new millennium. Changes in tax laws and the other positive outcomes we have discussed will enhance strong economic growth.

## 4. Third world nations will gain a middle class for the first time in history.

A few years ago, I traveled to Hong Kong and then to the interior of China where I discovered rampant poverty. A graphic view of what the cancerous system of communism does to a nation unfolded before my eyes.

China's future, however, will be brighter. As these proud people slowly open their country to the outside world, life for them will be changing from what they have known for centuries.

As I rode a bus up one of China's rural highways, I noticed that many huts along the way had freshly killed chickens hanging from porch rafters; the blood still dripping from the necks. Nearby, I saw large gates surrounded by manicured lawns announcing the entrance to mammoth factories built by some of America's most well-known companies. The huge parking lots were empty of cars. No one worked there; at least, not yet.

China appears poised to become the industrial center of the world, using Western technology and the millions of anxious Chinese workers.

What is keeping the gates closed? The repressive Chinese communist government. But its days are numbered. How will this affect you and me?

China — like other third world nations — has never before had a middle class. When manufacturing by American companies gets up and running on a large scale, the Chinese people will be working and making money. This new third world middle class will have cash to spend and guess what they will want to buy — everything Americans eat, drink, refrigerate, freeze, drive, write with, talk on, listen to, watch, and sleep on.

With hundreds of millions of people able to upgrade their living standard using Western products, our economy — and the economy of European and some Asian nations — could skyrocket for years to come.

Am I overly optimistic? I don't think so. The evidence points to prosperity.

## America's Future

I believe in a boom, not a bust. I think that is pretty clear whether you agree with me or not. I believe there are remarkable things ahead for Americans. I believe the quality of life in America will increase, not decrease as some would have us believe as we follow their desperate way of thinking. Here's how I see America's future:

Americans will enjoy greater income and more personal prosperity than their parents.

## A. The desire to succeed.

This drives them to succeed. As a result, the boomer generation will strive to improve not only their quality of life but also that of their children and grandchildren. That means prosperous and innovative times ahead for the next generations of Americans.

> *Several factors will help create this new wave of prosperity.*

This desire to succeed has resulted in an explosion of new entrepreneurs in corporate America; downsizing and manufacturing shut-downs have forced many middle-aged Americans to think of new ways to earn a living. As a result, they are starting their own small businesses, generating more income for themselves, and creating jobs for others. In fact, small businesses account for 80 percent of the jobs in the United States.

## B. More creative and fulfilling employment opportunities.

As discussed earlier, the emerging third world nations will supply the manpower needed to manufacture products. This will free up American workers to use their creative ingenuity to develop new goods and services required by their more financially secure countrymen. Other Americans will be able to concentrate on more skilled professions that pay a higher salary and provide more fulfilling and inspiring ways of earning an income.

The preachers of doom have worried about the coming robotic age; whining that millions will be unemployed because robots are more efficient, cheaper, and will replace American workers. This is hogwash. Robots are already taking the place of millions of humans in America and around the world, yet unemployment rates are stable.

In America, unemployment has been relatively low up to this recession. Why? Because of the creation of service-oriented companies in which robots cannot compete. This trend will continue as more innovative workers leave boring, mundane jobs and seek employment in growth industries that have positioned themselves toward meeting individual needs. As the recession weakens, the economic indicators become more positive, and unemployment statistics are one of those indicators that the economy is rebounding.

### C. The financial burden on families will be lifted.

Two inevitable changes will make this possible:

### 1. The income tax as we know it today will be abolished.

The present income tax laws are one of the main reasons why Americans are at risk of a financial collapse. Lower taxes mean higher growth and not the other way around.

### 2. Interest rates will drop.

Lower rates give more people the opportunity to qualify for a home mortgage. Sometimes 1 or 2 percentage points of interest on a home mortgage will keep a potential buyer from qualifying.

The lower rates coupled with reduced taxes and higher incomes will make purchasing a home affordable for more people. This is the reason when the economy does rebound, interest rates will stay low. The government will not want a repeat of the prime rates that were created to get people in homes, but a time bomb for home buyers when the balloon payments came due. Interest rates will be stable for the long term without the creative messes of the past.

### D. Lower inflation will reduce the need for two-income families.

In America today, most wives and mothers are forced to work just to pay the heavy tax burden levied on their families by inflation. Today, 60 percent of working mothers say, if given the choice, they would not work outside the home.

In years to came, inflation will remain low and stagnant. This will eliminate the need for two-income families.

### E. Families will have more discretionary income.

The added income from lowered taxes and increased income-producing opportunities will leave American families better off financially.

How will this additional income be spent?

### 1. To improve the quality of life for themselves and their families.

Once the necessities are taken care of, Americans inevitably turn to buying cars, boats, and the latest technology. Already, more luxury items are purchased by more Americans today than at any time in our nation's history. This trend will continue as Americans become richer.

Travel also increases as families have more money to spend on recreational activities and vacations. The ramifications of increased family spending are unending. Suffice it to say — construction of another Disney World is inevitable.

### 2. To save and make wise investments.

This trend will continue as more innovative workers leave boring, mundane jobs and seek employment in growth industries that have positioned themselves toward meeting individual needs.

Already, Americans are investing more of their money than at any other time in our nation's history. In fact, Americans are also better off today than ever as a whole –recession included. As opportunities arise, I predict that we will become even smarter investors and take greater advantage of the financial breaks created in the future.

As a result, people will be more prepared to handle financial setbacks, causing the bankruptcy rate to decline. Investment spending will also increase as new retirement vehicles are developed and the government gets out of the Social Security business.

Children will grow up knowing their parents are setting aside money, not only for college, but also funds that can be used to start a business or launch a career.

### F. Companies will change the way they do business.

These changes will affect not only the companies themselves but also the buying habits of American consumers.

### Smaller will be better.

The NASDAQ stock market will rise and become nearly as large as the New York Stock Exchange. The reason? Because opportunities exist for small businesses to make profits. Entrepreneurship moves a free market economy. You perhaps cannot see this now, but read this chapter in five years.

In the 1970s and 1980s, consolidation was the trend. Bigger companies were swallowing up smaller ones through takeovers and leveraged buy-outs. In the future, these companies will be selling off their subsidiaries and digressing from the way they have done business in the past. This trend will unleash salary and wage increases presently locked up by powerful work forces.

**Products will be more specialized.**

Americans are developing a preference for customization as the increase in specialty retail shops indicates. As baby boomers demand more specialized products, companies will move away from standard assembly line production. High quality products are the wave of the future.

Already, I receive stacks of magazines featuring specialized products that are more expensive but of much higher quality than average mass-produced goods. New technology will make these customized items affordable for even the average income person.

**Products will be sold through different mediums.**

The popularity of catalog purchasing along with shopping networks on the Internet is already changing the way America shops. People will more and more like the convenience of shopping from home and having goods delivered directly to their doors.

**Americans will alter their lifestyles; more people will work from home.**

Home computers, fax machines, and the Internet make it possible for many Americans to work from a home office. The expansion of home-based businesses in the last five years has been phenomenal, generating a flurry of new entrepreneurs. That trend has not slowed an inch during this recession and, if anything, has expanded as people in trouble look for ways to increase their incomes.

Aside from the convenience, working from home is more economical; saving gas mileage, business clothes, and daily lunch expenses.

**Women will have more choices.**

With the reduced tax burden, mothers will be able to stay home and raise their children if they so choose. Older women who do not feel the need to work will become involved in church, charitable, and community activities. As a result, this new force of concerned citizens will help make positive social changes in their neighborhoods and cities.

Women who decide to enter the workforce will make more money and be more highly skilled. From the late 1980s to the present, the number of women–owned businesses in all sectors has increased substantially, and this trend is bound to continue in years to come.

Many women will choose the best of both worlds and decide to operate innovative home-based businesses, taking advantage of the changes in computer technology and Internet access to world markets.

### Rural living will become more popular.

A migration from big city life is already in progress. More professionals like me prefer to live in small rural areas as opposed to the large cities. It's "in" to live in the country.

Suburbs were originally created to escape high taxation imposed by inner-city governments. Since land on the outside was cheaper, suburbs were born, and families fled the urban nightmare of traffic, crime, and smog.

Instead of moving to the suburbs, however, younger families are discovering the benefits of living in small towns. In fact, many factories, in an effort to avoid paying high union wages, are relocating to smaller cities and towns, especially in the South.

This trend will grow even stronger if our cities continue to deteriorate with increases in crime, violence, and taxes.

### Economic shifts will occur among the world's Super Powers.

Let's look at how changes in the United States, Europe, Russia, and Japan will affect one another.

### 1. The United States will continue to be the undisputed world power.

America's power will result from our economic stability, our superior technical skills, and our quality education. As the more educated and skilled generation of boomers take over the leadership roles of America, our greatness as a nation will emerge.

Positions once held by members of the older generation will be filled with boomers who have come of age in their late 40s, 50s and 60s, The benefits from this new wave of positive leadership could continue for the next 20 to 40 years.

### 2. The economies of the European nations will emerge.

Europe and the United States will become even more economically tied than in the past. This economic unity will benefit all the European nations. As the Eastern bloc countries become strong democracies, they will move quickly toward a more Westernized culture and greater prosperity. Their citizens will have the money to purchase imported American products.

### 3. Russia will become economically stable.

Eventually, Russia will formulate a free market economy that is not controlled by crooks and black marketers. Using their gold reserves, Russia's leaders will stabilize their economy.

As the Russians finally move into the 21st century, their economic and technological growth will mean that more foreign companies will locate there. This will benefit the U.S. and European economies, which will flood Russia with cars, refrigerators, clothes, televisions, and technology.

### 4. Japan's financial bubble will burst.

Since 1988, Japan has experienced more than a dozen stock market downturns. I believe, as do others, that Japan's wealth is proportioned greatly by paper and nothing else. Japan's real estate market, which is already on shaky ground, will probably collapse sometime in the next decade.

As a protectionist state, Japan's camouflage will eventually fade and affect its economic growth. Any nation with $12 hamburgers and $600 ski lift tickets signals a dangerous ring at the cash register.

## Changes Are Coming

Is my analysis of the economy too optimistic? Some people think so. Why? Because they compare Americans to the Romans, Greeks, Babylonians, Caledonians, and every other "ite" and "ian" in history. These naysayers claim we are going the way of other now extinct societies who, as a result of becoming fat, lazy, despondent, lackadaisical and rich, finally self-destructed.

As far as I'm concerned, that is like comparing Benjamin Franklin, the great orator and inventor, to a Hollywood starlet who can't keep a husband. The two are vastly different yet both are powerful, famous, and wealthy in their own right.

The previously mentioned cultures were pagan. There is a vast difference in people and nations whose complete psychological and spiritual nature rests in polytheism and ruthless pagan worship. No culture will ever last whose sole hope and trust is in something they have made with their own hands. The Judeo-Christian cultures have already endured longer than any pagan empire.

If our country were to embrace the New Age philosophies, and these pagan ideas were to become the norm for our spiritual guidance and leadership, then I would have to agree that our whole society is doomed. You only have to visit India to see what paganism can do to a country. People floating into space and having out-of-body experiences are not the normal habits of clear-thinking progressives.

I don't believe our country is any way near wholeheartedly embracing neo-paganism. In fact, I see a conservative movement strengthening across the land, but offer a word of caution: The more non-Christian cultures we allow to reside in the country, the more danger we are of becoming in judgment, such as Israel was in the Old Testament.

For 40 years, we lived under the iron fist of liberalism — a philosophy that created many of our nation's social problems. Political permissiveness has almost ruined this great land.

Changes are coming, however, and those changes will affect every phase of our lives — social, spiritual, and economic. America is no longer divided on moral issues but is ready and willing to unite and dismantle the socialistic policies of the welfare state — ideas that didn't work. We were sold a bill of goods for many years, and it wasn't until Ronald Reagan took office that the sleeping giant of conservatism was finally awakened.

Conservatives have learned a valuable lesson with the election of Barack Hussein Obama. If you go to sleep and lose your priorities, anything can happen. But, I believe liberal heads will once again roll across the nation, and a clear mandate for conservative government leadership will be our salvation. Trust me: the liberals of this nation fear that political resurrection more than they fear any one thing.

My optimism doesn't lie in a "pie in the sky" philosophy. It rests in the belief that the baby boomers of my generation — who are the largest voting bloc in the country — are ready to take back America.

America's economic problems will not destroy us — our immorality will. If we take control of our morals, the other problems will take care of themselves. Listen, the economy will take care of its own woes; the lack of morals will destroy the nation.

Putting all the positives together creates a pretty picture of the future. There are a lot of reasons to be optimistic.

## Bullish On America

In my library, I probably have every major financial book ever written. All of them have a common topic: how to survive in a financial crisis. I have a different goal for this book. I prefer advising you on how to take a few risks as a way of properly preparing you for a prosperous future.

Americans have been so brainwashed into negative thinking that many consider it abnormal to be upbeat and positive. As a result, few people offer any solutions to our problems since they consider our nation already doomed.

My purpose is not to get you prepared for a so-called "underground economy" full of the boogie bears. Neither do I recommend sewing up your investments so tight that experiencing any real growth becomes impossible. I don't ignore the fact that some kind of downturn or economic fallout is possible. Such events are inevitable, and you can count on them. But nobody knows when that will happen. My goal is to convince you of a bright future and prepare you to be in a position to take advantage of it.

How many times have you told yourself, or heard someone say, "I wish I had done this 20, 30, 40 years ago"?

I said that myself just a few weeks ago in one of our advisory meetings. As I looked around the room at the young people I have working under me, I wished I had been exposed to the same opportunities they have today when I was in my late 20s.

In our country, the avenues of opportunity are always open. The time frame makes no difference except when you are fine-tuning your venture.

When Peter Lynch was asked when was a good time to invest in the stock market, he replied, "Any time."

As time goes on, the same opportunities for solid investment in the stock market will be there in the future just as the future was being made in the past.

In the late 1960s, the flower children sat crossed-legged at Woodstock smoking their brains out and singing about trees dying from air pollution. These hippies never dreamed that 30 years later the air would actually be cleaner and trees could be grown eight times faster than nature had ever produced them before.

Many of those same hippies are doctors, lawyers, and stock brokers today enjoying the good life and living in redwood houses and walking on oak floors. Sure they probably recycle their newspapers and plastic — as we all should. Practicing conservation not only preserves our natural resources but helps the economy. After all, environmental concerns have spawned many new industries and led to the creation of useful and innovative products.

I am bullish on America because the same spirit that made this country great in the beginning is alive and well today. Like our forefathers, Americans are pioneering new territories in space, technology, manufacturing, pharmaceuticals, and energy sources. If you can envision it, someone is probably on the verge of patenting it.

But there is another reason I am convinced there will be a big boom in the economy in the near future.

## The Dawn of Change

An economic and social boom awaits America, and many legislative proposals are poised to enhance this explosion. Policy changes are coming because the survival of America — or at least the enhancement of the country — depends upon it.

But we're not out of the woods yet. Danger still lurks in the shadows to disembowel any attempt to regain our sanity as a country.

It took years for America to get us in the mess we find ourselves today, and it will take a while to get out. As voters, we must pay attention to the issues that affect our nation's economic and social future.

You and I need to put pressure on our elected officials to do what is best for our nation. Americans can no longer allow congressional leaders to have a free hand to pass legislation unchecked. As voting citizens, we must hold them accountable for their actions.

Although I went to law school, I believe we should stop electing lawyers to political positions and instead put more businessmen who understand the economy into office. In fact, most of the positive legislative changes that have been instituted in the past few years have been birthed by politicians who are not lawyers.

Entrenched politicians lose touch with reality. We need to restrict the number of years elected officials can serve. As more and more states enforce term limits, Congress will eventually be forced to comply. In the end, term limits will be right for America.

Until November 1995, our government was held captive by a liberal Congress who nearly bankrupted us. The embracing of socialism and welfarism by our so-called capitalist leadership put our nation in jeopardy. In spite of the 40-year rule by tax-and-spend congressional Democrats, America's free market economic system survived — and even thrived under Ronald Reagan.

So what happened? In 2009, we're strapped by some of the same Congressional Democrats that bled us prior to Newt Gingrich and the 95th Congress. Republicans and America messed up.

Finally, America will once again have the opportunity to break the stronghold of liberalism in Congress and in the presidency. The dawn of

*America's Insurance Policy is freedom. When men are free, they produce.*

change looms bright on the horizon if true patriots take back the leadership and control of this country, and the liberals are returned to their law practices.

During the 19th and 20th centuries, freedom has been assaulted on every hand. Countries once free as they left the late 1800s were enslaved by World War II. Nazism, Fascism, and Communism captured a large portion of the world. Freedom dimmed in the 20th Century.

As the dawn is breaking early in the 21st Century, changes will have taken place that began in the 1980s when Ronald Reagan took office. The totalitarian systems that threatened us for decades today have no power. Socialism has failed, and communism has been overthrown throughout the world.

Can anything ensure the economic future of the United States from collapse? Yes. Freedom.

When America's freedom of ownership is once again protected

from political sabotage, we will return to pure capitalism and a free market economy. When men are free, they produce.

Clarence B. Carson in his book, *Basic Economics,* quotes a lecture by Ludwig von Mises, a leader of the Austrian school of economics:

"The capitalist system was termed capitalism not by a friend of the system, but by an individual who considered it to be the worst of all historical systems, the greatest evil that had ever befallen mankind. That man was Karl Marx."

Nevertheless, there is no reason to reject Marx's term because it describes clearly the source of the great social improvements brought about by capitalism. These improvements are the result of capital accumulation. They are based on the fact that people, as a rule, do not consume everything they have produced; that they save and invest — part of it.

Prosperity will come when our government enacts laws that preserve our economic freedom. Why is that important? Because the results of economic freedom are:

**1. Free enterprise**

**2. Free markets**

**3. Freedom of trade**

**4. Private ownership of property**

When a society prospers, an added bonus follows: many social and moral ills are cured.

Take away private capital, and you have destroyed freedom. What is the first act of a dictator after he seizes control of a nation? He takes away the rights of the people to unlimited private ownership and use of capital.

As Americans, we get angry at the way our government spends our tax dollars. Few other topics create more debate, hot tempers, and disgust. We can kick and yell all we want but at least we can kick and yell!

In America, we can do something about how the government spends money that belongs to us. As long as we have that freedom, the propensity for a prosperous future will belong to all Americans for a long time to come. But only as long as we are free.

Finally, my best friend and partner, Jim Johnson of Reno, Nevada, who reads every book I produce before it is ever seen by anyone else, finished this book. Jim and Cris are involved in marriage seminars and counseling through *Enjoying Marriage of Nevada.*

Jim opined to me that he had read the book, but it is missing one key ingredient: How do you avoid listening to and being influenced by the hundreds of emails that bombard your Internet service concerning doomsday scenarios?

My first thought was: *"Try not listening to doomsday junk for six weeks and see how it affects you."*

"No, no," Jim replied, "You need to produce a Doomsday test so that people can sort out if what they are reading and listening to is affecting them."

"How so?" I asked.

"Before the last election, I turned off all the media and refused to listen to all the negative stuff being preached concerning our nation's demise if Obama was not elected. I immediately started feeling less frustrated and could actually sleep at night," Jim explained.

"What about my saying that anything that contradicts what I am writing about in this book is doomsayer influences," I remarked.

"That's a cop-out," Jim said. "Somebody needs to tell people it is okay to not read or listen to this stuff for hours on end. You wrote the book; do it. Never before have I read anything that says, *'It's okay to stop reading the junk.'"*

To determine the effect of Doomsday influences, take this simple test.

Is what I am reading and listening to:

• Causing me anxiety?
• Making me want to pull in my horns because I am being sold fear?
• Making me want to give up instead of fight?
• Making me afraid for my family and friends?
• Controlling my central faith in God?
• Causing me to lose control of the peace in my life?

If you have one of these thoughts, you are being influenced by negative and destructive information.

The media has made a living selling fear. In this time, it is more than the media selling the junk that causes sleepless nights and anxieties God never intended for his children. People are past depression; they are in despair.

My favorite movie of all time is *Anne of Green Gables*. I know every line in that movie. My favorite line from any movie occurs when Anne is trying to sort out some troublesome spots in her life. She is behind Morella, her adopted aunt, as they are moving up the stairs.

"I am in the depths of despair," Anne opines to Morella.

"You're not in despair, Anne." Morella complains. "To despair is to turn your back on God."

There you have it. I am writing about the effects of a tasteless philosophy that has no common sense, no practical application, and turns its back on the God of the universe who controls it all anyway. Yet, I do not read one single thing the doomsayers are preaching, and I get emails from all over the world trying to influence my thinking.

I will not "turn my back on God," so I am instructing you to follow this advice instead of believing every scary story that will take away the peace and tranquility God intends for your life.

# CHAPTER ELEVEN

# IF I COULD DO IT ALL OVER AGAIN

Who hasn't said — or at least thought — *"If I could only do it all over again, I would do things differently."*

Since no one is perfect, we could all make some things in our lives better if we could go back and redo them.

Peering into the past can be scary. Reviewing all the mistakes we have made can be downright depressing; especially if we dwell on "what might have been." Still, such an exercise can be beneficial — especially for those who come behind us. Given a second chance, I would do some things differently.

Experience has taught me enough lessons the hard way, and I do not want my children, grandchildren, family members, friends, and my readership to be educated by the same school of "hard knocks." While examples from my own life could alone fill a book, I have chosen to single out a few important things I would do if I could live my life over. This list comprises what I feel are the most important practices that if missed can cause anyone to fall way short of their financial potential.

Tom Mills, an investment advisor in Napa, California, wrote a column called *Common Cents* for the local paper. He published a similar list and made an interesting comment. "Many clients and friends tell me what they would do if they could live their lives over," Mills wrote. "The usual list includes spending more time with their children, not taking life so seriously, telling their spouse how much they love them, exercising more, and concentrating on their education, etc."

After reading Mills' list, I decided to take my own poll of clients and friends and document their answers to this question: "If you could do things over again, what would you do that you didn't do the first time?"

Many people focused on the social aspects of life; like going to church more regularly — or starting to church in the first place. "Getting an education and spending more time applying myself" was a common response from those who wished their lives were more productive.

Have you ever thought how much better your life would be if you had made different financial decisions?

This book has dealt with the stresses certain financial pressures cause. When life goes sour, many times the results can be traced to a decision we made concerning money. Life is full of choices, and many of us have less in the end because we did not make good choices in the beginning.

The way we handle our finances has a lot to do with what we become, how successful we are, and the outcome of our lives. In the end will we have enough money? This depends: will we run out of time before we do money, or run out of money before we do time? This is an important question. I wish I had been asked this during my college days.

Our entire happiness in the golden years of our lives may depend on our income. In fact, the end result of our financial reserves is a product of the choices we made in the beginning. Bad decisions that lead to financial chaos make it extremely difficult to recoup later and live normally.

Those who responded to my poll and answered my question told me what they would do if they could do it all over again. Here are their ten most common responses:

## 1. I Would Save Money

This response was number one on everyone's list. People look back over the years and think about all the money they spent on things they no longer have or need. Most of us waste a lot of money.

During your lifetime, you are going to earn a lot of money. Whether that will be enough money depends on how you spend it. If we are honest, most of us can testify that we have not spent our money gradually. Instead, we have handed it over in bundles when we desperately wanted a particular item; not waiting before we spend is a bad habit. I preach a lot to myself about impulse buying, yet I'm still doing it.

I purchased a 1957 Chevy two-door coupe from one of my golfing buddies — who also happens to be my chiropractor. I tell him he gets in my pocket during the golf game and afterward on the adjustment table. He got into it again by selling me his car. Being the sucker I am, I bought his antique Chevy so he could purchase a new Harley Davidson motorcycle. We were both turning 50 years old and decided we would treat ourselves to something special. He could afford it, I could not.

Why do we spend money to satisfy emotional needs? How much money would most of us have if we did not waste so much? I am not advocating being a miser. My father taught me that money is to spend and hoarding it can make you just as miserable as not having any.

Through the years, I have enjoyed my money and purchased many things I wanted — and some things I didn't — but as I look back, I must admit I should have saved more and bought less. That is one thing I would definitely do differently if given the opportunity.

I would have postponed buying many of the material things I purchased. Why? Because they kept me miserable trying to pay for them while watching them deteriorate into nothingness. If I had waited and saved the money, I could have bought the same things with the interest I would have earned.

As Americans, we're afraid of dying before we can enjoy all the stuff that advertisers say we need. Therefore we spend. Like most people my age, I am still working to make money when I should be relaxing more.

Someday we'll all grow up. My hope and prayer is we'll do it before we run out of money. Why wait until it's too late? It's much easier to learn to live within your means now. If you do, you can put some money aside each week toward your future instead of regretting wasting your income.

While writing this book, I decided to experiment with myself concerning saving. During the months of working to complete this project, I pitched my change each night into a big jar sitting beside my dresser. After this project was completed, I had saved more than $600 in loose change. If I had started saving my loose change 30 years ago, I would have amassed $24,000 in loose change plus interest. Instead, most of those coins were gobbled by soda machines, making PepsiCo richer instead of me.

If you smoke a pack of cigarettes a day and pay $4.50 per pack, it costs you $135 per month or $1,620 a year. After 30 years, if you live that long, you will have spent $48,600 plus interest committing suicide. If you had invested that money exponentially over time, it could easily be three or four times this much.

I believe in enjoying life, but we could do without many things in order to have more of the things we cannot do without. There is an old saying, "There are those who pay interest, and there are those who earn it." The best way to make the most of our money is to save some of it.

## 2. I Would Adopt the Attitude that Quality Is the Best Policy

It costs only a little more to go first class.

One of life's great pleasures is owning things that have value. In my life, I have bought a lot of junk. The junk didn't last long and is not even a memory in my mind.

Many of the items I did buy when I went first class are still around because they lasted. Sometimes it costs a little more, but you will get more pleasure out of a few nice things than you will out of lot of junk.

Clothes are a good example. Purchasing cheap business suits and replacing them eventually ends up costing more than springing for one nice suit that always retains its shape and gives a good appearance. There are few exceptions to this, as anyone who goes for quality knows.

One of the men who worked in our financial firm bought several expensive, tailor-made dress shirts in San Francisco. He could only afford three or four of them, but everyone in our office was envious of how neat he looked. His shirts outlasted to one any cheaper model. In fact, he still has those shirts, and after a few years of wear, they look as if they will last a few more.

As a financial advisor, he says it was cheaper to go with the tailor-made quality of a fine shirt. The same can be said for shoes, coats, ties, wallets — anything that gets a lot of wear.

Furniture, appliances, and other household items that are expensive to repair or replace will always serve you better, and cost less, in the long run if you purchase high-quality brand names.

### 3. I Would Go to a Professional for Financial Advice

If I had it to do over, I would not have relied on my own reasoning to determine how to invest or manage my money. Now that I am a professional in this area, I understand the importance of getting advice.

King Solomon told us it is wise to seek counsel. Huge financial mistakes are made regularly by people who will not seek the advice of professionals to handle every day money problems.

You would not diagnose your own medical problems or handle your own legal issues, would you? Why then do you try to handle your own investment problems? Wise counsel by qualified people is crucial to reaching your financial goals unless you have a lot of money to waste    which most of us don't.

I am always unraveling messes people have made of their finances — and I have made a few of my own. If I had it to do again, I would have called an investment advisor, made an appointment, and told him my present financial state, shared where I wanted to go, and then done exactly what he told me.

If I had done what I am now telling other people to do, I would be a lot richer and possibly more financially secure.

### 4. I Would Go Into Business at Least Once

A lot of people would love to get into business for themselves. Perhaps they have an idea they want to try, or have a skill they want to convey and make money while doing it. Although being in business has its pitfalls, it still remains a large part of the American dream.

For many Americans, multi-level marketing opportunities have fulfilled the vision of owning their own business. Why is multi-level marketing so successful? Because it provides an outlet for people to make money by their own resources without investing a lot of capital.

People are home marketing everything from soap powder to yachts. Vitamins, weight loss programs, and skin care products are the most popular and have the largest market share. In the future, almost everything will be available through home marketing businesses.

Many people, however, get into business, do not belong there, and fail. Still, they have tried, and that is the fulfillment of a dream. Others start off moonlighting then become very successful and are able to quit the boring day job they have hated for years.

When out of frustration people call me and ask how they can make ends meet, I always tell them, "Look for alternate ways to make money."

Great opportunities exist in America, and more and more people need to take advantage of them. If you are willing to put in the time, there are many ways to earn extra income. Opportunities in this country abound. Look for them.

### 5. I Would Take More Chances in My Youth

Youth only comes once; it flies away quickly and can never be reclaimed.

I wish as a young man, I had gone out on a limb more often while I had the time to recover. Although I probably took more chances than most people, as I look back, I should have taken more.

This may appear reckless but let me explain. I have traveled to many foreign nations and witnessed the oppression under which many people live. Foreigners are beating down America's door to get at the opportunities afforded us every day. As a citizen of the United States, I have realized that being overly cautious borders on foolishness.

America was settled by millions of immigrants who risked everything to come to this country and enjoy the freedom our Republican form of government offers — the privilege of owning property and starting a business. That dream is still here. Most immigrants migrating to America today are not only coming to escape tyranny, but also to find a lifestyle that is unprecedented in the history of the world.

You only have to visit a university campus to realize the number of foreign students taking advantage of America's educational opportunities. An immigrant from Hungary who had come here to join his family told me he was in love with America long before he ever got here.

I will never forget the comment he made to me one day: "I became disillusioned very quickly over here," he said. "What is wrong with these people?"

No nation on the planet affords to everyday, common people the opportunities for employment and prosperity that Americans enjoy. Many, however, have abused that privilege, and others don't bother to put forth the effort needed to take advantage of the educational and vocational opportunities available to anyone who wants to succeed.

The work ethic of many Japanese, Vietnamese, and Chinese immigrants puts many Americans to shame. Do you know that Korean families who immigrated to the United States in the past 20 years earn a higher income than the average American family?

Who cannot be amazed at Cuban and Haitian immigrants who travel in make-shift crafts across treacherous, shark-infested waters to fulfill their dreams and reach the shores of "the land of the free and the home of the brave"?

What would you have to risk to reach for your dreams? I doubt that it would be a life or death decision.

If I had it to do over again, I would take more chances and pursue every possibility.

### 6. I Would Postpone Gratification

I would not have taken the short cut many times and instead would have stuck it out for the long term. Although I am referring to investments, this principle could apply to every area of life. Many times we take the easy way out, and that costs us in the end.

I would have paid my dues up front and gotten my education early in life, making every effort to do so. I was fortunate to enter a profession that allowed me to get back into school later in life. Someone had said, "Get the education first; the money will come later."

Instead of a buying a new house and car, as I did, I would have sacrificed to take the time to finish college. I made a big mistake by not completing my education as a young man before taking on all the responsibilities of marriage and family.

Most of the people in life's pressure cooker have taken this same route. They neglect the learning processes of life and must settle for less-than-complete satisfaction because it is too late.

## 7. I Would Make a Long-term Plan

I would make a plan not only financially but for everything I intended to do. Why? Because there is a difference between a pipe dream and a vision.

Pipedreams are conjured up by "wannabes" who are always chasing the pot of gold at the end of the rainbow. Visionaries take action in life and work toward achieving their goals. They are never satisfied until they meet their desired objective.

Remember the question I ask potential employees of my firm? "When you get where you are going, where will you be?"

It is good to have goals, but how do we get where we want to be? Implementing the steps needed to accomplish our dreams and goals is another matter.

Years ago, when our family decided to drive across America for the first time, we didn't just jump into the car, put it car in drive, and press the accelerator, being led around by happenstance. We had a plan.

I checked the maps to see how to get across the United States. I outlined the exact routes I would take. I paid strict attention to the road signs as I was driving along, making sure that I knew precisely what exits to take and which highways to follow to my destination.

I checked the map often — every night and at stops along the way — to make sure we were still headed in the right direction.

I had a timetable. I knew approximately how long it would take me to get where I was going.

I had estimated the costs, so I wouldn't run out of money.

The next time we drove across the country and back, I was able to duplicate the trip, staying in the same hotels, stopping at the same gas stations, and eating at the same restaurants. Although the journey took two weeks, we arrived within two hours of the time it took us on the first trip! Everyone was impressed — including me.

If I could go back and do 'life' over, I would have been as efficient with my time, my money, and my goals as I was with the planning of that trip.

## 8. I Would Avoid Risky Ventures

I deal with people all the time who have risked their money without having any control over it. (They've wished they could do it all over again.) Many fortunes have been lost on wildcat strikes and dried-up holes. There is no fortune to be had in quicksand.

Taking chances by your own volition and determination is one thing, but getting into a deal with someone else without knowing much about it is quite another. I am not talking about taking chances when you have the control and have made the decision as to how you believe things will turn out. I am talking about making investment decisions when you do not know the risks you are taking.

Earlier in the book I mentioned some 1980s doomsayer financial advisors who thought the world would blow up by the end of that decade. They were convinced the price of oil would be so high that America would be a great place to invest in oil exploration. They encouraged their constituents to place their money in oil wells in Texas and Oklahoma, among others.

Sure, there is oil in Texas and in Oklahoma. Rockefeller built his empire out of the fortunes he found under American soil. The oil is still there, but the demand isn't. As a result, thousands of investors who followed the doomsayer's advice suffered tremendous financial loss when an oil glut occurred and caused the price of oil to fall.

Why did many innocent people lose money? Because they didn't know the risks involved. Instead of taking the advice of radio and television advisors, they should have sought out a professional who could inform them of the pros and cons of such an investment.

Today, people get taken in by charlatans who buy time on the radio and use scare tactics to entice the uninformed into buying rare coins or gold bouillon. If you are tempted to go that route, make sure you get the advice of a financial investment professional before you mail anyone your hard-earned money.

## 9. I Would Give My Kids More Time

Would you have given your kids more material things while they were growing up? Those from this school of thought feel guilty that their children grew up without the clothes and toys to compete with other kids who had more than they did. They think their children were not happy.

I gave my kids most of what they wanted but never enough to spoil them. What would I do differently if I had to do it over? Give them more of myself. They not only missed out, but so did I. I am fortunate because my two boys grew up, went to college, earned their degrees, and for a long time worked with me every day at my firm. During those years, I spent more time with them than I did while they were growing up. It was fun, and I realized all the great times we could have had together when they were boys. Today, they are in their own careers and have families, but I greatly miss those days I could visit with them, work with them, and enjoy their company.

Someone once said to me, "Kids are no reason for two people to stay together." I disagree. The kids are the exact reason two people should stay together. If a husband and wife have problems, they should put those on the back burner while raising the children.

While couples are trying to find their own identities in life, it is the children who suffer. Unless the kids are harmed by a violent and disturbing relationship between two people, the parents should stay together for the sake of the children.

## 10. I Would Pay More Attention to My Problems

My father used to say, "If you don't handle your problems, your problems will handle you." Failing to handle issues as they arise is a serious mistake.

I am often asked, "What is the one piece of advice you could give that would solve most of the financial problems that businesses, families, and institutions have in common?"

Although a difficult question with a variety of answers, this is probably the single best response I could give: Never be afraid to quit.

In other words, there is nothing wrong with quitting when you need to stop. It takes courage to face failure. Many hardships in life could be averted if people would realize their backs are against the wall and stop beating their heads against it.

When a situation has no future, it's time to pull in the horns, chalk up your losses, and either start over or move on.

I once had a partner who put it this way: "Take care of the little bills, and the big bills will take care of themselves."

It is difficult to deal with every problem that can happen in life. When I have finished this book, a hundred different issues will probably come to mind that I did not cover and wish I had mentioned. That is part of life.

John Lennon once said, "Life interferes with all the things you want to do."

I love to play golf. It took years of playing before I broke into the 70s for the first time. When I did, one of my golfing friends said, "I don't believe I know anyone who has worked as hard on the game of golf as Sherm Smith."

"I wish I had worked as hard at life as I have learning how to play golf," I said.

Golf is a game, but life isn't. Sometimes I believe we take our games much more seriously than we do living. Financial situations creep up on us. We do not get into financial trouble overnight; it takes time.

## Five Common Financial Predicaments

Seventy-six percent of the people I have talked to about what they would do differently say that economic difficulties are their number one problem. Most of them were able to isolate five common financial predicaments.

1. Not having enough money
2. Addicted to spending
3. Unable to handle credit
4. Trying to buy acceptance
5. Giving money away

Let's look at each of these and discuss how to fix them:

### 1. Not Having Enough Money

Money is not a problem until you don't have enough, and then it becomes a big problem. How do you solve it? Read this book again.

Have you ever heard someone say, "I don't have any money problems money can't solve?" Although that is a well-worn cliché, in many ways it is the truth. Most of the things we need in life take money to get them. The rest of our needs are emotional, but even they are often tied to money.

The next time someone says to you, "Money is the least important thing in my life," reply, "I don't believe you."

In reality, money solves a lot of problems because most problems were created by a lack of money in the first place. In the end, problems can get out of control because we don't have the money to resolve them.

How can you attack the problem of not having enough money? By simply working at it. Take all the things you have learned in this and other money management books and apply them to your situation. If you have to start over, carefully document the areas where you went wrong to avoid the mistakes you made the first time around.

### 2. Addicted to Spending

Most people who have money problems have them because they cannot control their spending. I have offered examples in this writing of people who got out of control and nearly ruined themselves financially — or actually did.

The problem of spending too much can be controlled rather easily with some safeguards — like a budget. Why? Because advertisers target people with the weakness to spend. Some people are addicted to spending the way others are addicted to drinking too much, smoking too much, eating too much, or gambling too much. They have uncontrollable urges to spend.

As a boy, when I would earn some cash and immediately spend it, my mother would tell me, "That money was burning a hole in your pocket!"

Money is a beguiling temptation, and some people cannot control the burning urge to buy things with it. People who have an addiction to spending don't necessarily have a great love for money, nor are they obsessed with earning it. Their problem is they have no control once they get money. Anything they desire suddenly becomes a major issue, and the resources they have in their pocket or bank accounts are used to satisfy any latent material urges.

If a person refuses to acknowledge their problem, then Bible-based counseling may be necessary to bring it to the forefront. A spending problem, although severe, can be solved. However, the solutions are not simple and take discipline. Having enough money throughout life means a consecrated control of spending.

Spending habits are created by material desires. Intoxicated by the desire to possess material things, a person can lose all sense of reason. I know the feeling, and so do you. Just the thought of buying something new, whether we need it or not, can send waves of exhilaration up and down the spine.

What happens when you have wanted something for a long time? As soon as you get some money, you forget the priorities you had listed on your goal sheet and splurge on the desired item. Instead of spending the money on something you really need or on your monthly obligations, you only worsen your present financial problems.

To determine if you have a slight, obsessive spending problem, take this test on your next vacation. While you are driving around looking for a hotel, see if you can resist the desire for a "room with a view" in lieu of a cheaper one that looks out on the parking lot. You'll be surprised by how much money you can save if you postpone looking at the ocean — or the mountain peaks — until the next morning when you can see it in daylight for free.

What about the restaurants where you eat while on vacation? Do you select a fancy restaurant every night or just once in a while?

Spending is not wrong as long as you have the expenses covered in your budget. People who cannot afford excessive spending and are in trouble because of it need to check their motives constantly. Being short of money is predicated by how you choose to use it.

### 3. Unable to Handle Credit

In my wallet, I have credit cards with $40,000 limits. You can imagine the temptation that presents!

Thousands of people cannot handle credit — even more cannot handle credit card debt. This epidemic has resulted from the relative ease with which people with good credit can obtain credit cards.

In the past, banks used to lend money predicated upon something of value used as collateral. Today, banks compete for our credit dollars and determine a person's credibility by the way he or she pays other credit card bills.

It's not unusual to receive credit cards in the mail without even asking for them. All you have to do is sign the application and send it in. Many of these cards offer $2,500 to $5,000 credit lines.

Imagine a married couple who has never had that much credit before, or who had to go physically to the bank and borrow the money with a good excuse. The hassle of doing this and being turned down was not palatable, so they never bothered. Now, when faced with the temptation to purchase something they want, this couple charges it on the credit card, choosing to pay for it later. As a result, they get in over their heads and before long they are drowning in interest payments.

At one point, I ran my credit cards to the hilt. Fearing that my good credit rating would be jeopardized by too much credit, I paid down the balances as far as I could — which wasn't all that much. Instead of affecting my credit negatively, every credit card company raised my balances!

Overspending is the financial problem in America that will leave many people penniless unless they get help.

**To fight the overspending habit you must:**

A. **Control credit cards or cut them up.**

B. **Have no more than two cards. This will save you money in annual card fees.**

C. **Have a strict budget and discipline yourself to stick to it.**

D. **Keep account of all expenses.**

E. **Let someone take care of all your money for a while until you feel you have some control.**

F. **Limit your buying to one or two items every six months, and then only buy if you have saved the money to purchase them.**

G. **Don't charge anything on credit cards until you have paid them off.**

H. **Pay the balance on every card every month.**

Let's face it. Banks want us to use their credit cards, and there is nothing wrong with the convenience they provide. But in terms of the interest we pay for all that privilege, we should be careful of falling into the "minimum payment" trap. Remember, the only people getting rich on credit cards are the banks who issue them.

## Peer Pressure

In 1987, Fortune magazine printed an article titled, The Money Society, which described the mood of the 1980s:

"Money, money, money is the incantation of today. Bewitched by an epidemic of money enchantment, Americans in the eighties wriggle in a St. Vitas dance of materialism unseen since the Gilded Age or the Roaring Twenties. Under the blazing sum of money, all other values shine palely."

"I think people are being measured again by money rather than by how good a journalist or social activist or lawyer they are," says an investment banker. "It frightens me to be sensitive to the idea that my neighbor just got a big screen TV that's three inches bigger than mine," says the banker. "I think the stress and internal turmoil that creates in most of us is unhealthy."

Since the time this article was first printed in 1987, America's lust for materialism has grown worse. Today, in the late 2000s, many believe that prosperity is the key to happiness and acceptability. The motivational gurus tell us we have to look successful in order to be successful.

Our quest to have money in order to impress one another has caused our entire culture to hide behind an opaque curtain from which we almost never venture unless we are shocked into it. We are becoming a society very skilled at hiding our true selves. The reason? Peer pressure.

How can we cure the prosperity problem? By understanding the real value of love and friendship. True friends are not bought. You don't have to give them things to buy their love. They will care for you whether you have or have not.

A true relationship is built upon the value of who a person is, not what a person has. I like the way someone put it many years ago: "A true friend knows your faults but loves you anyway." Material things do not enter into the equation.

The only reason you need material things is to make your life more comfortable and enjoyable. Running yourself into debt by buying things to impress people is foolish.

## Giving Money Away

Many of my clients are good, Christian people. In fact, most Americans consider themselves in this category.

---
### Worship Is Not Complete Until You Have Given To God
---

Almost every Judeo-Christian person in America has been taught that they should give to God out of their incomes each Sunday. Baptists, Catholics, Methodists, Presbyterians, Lutherans, Episcopalians, Pentecostals, Nazarenes, Seventh-Day Adventists, Mormons, Jehovah Witnesses, and Jews believe that 10 percent of their income should be given to support their respective churches.

It is a common belief that tithing is taught in the Bible, and we are obligated to practice it. I support this belief and exercise it myself. In fact, you may sing, pray, teach a class, and sing in the choir, but you haven't finished worshipping until you have given to God what belongs to Him. Since there are so many church-related people in this nation, it is impossible to ignore the fact that many people are caught up in the idea that if they keep giving to God, He will pour out His blessings upon them and they "shall not want."

Although it is not my intention to go into the theological aspects of this belief and practice, I must say the skeleton of the idea is divine Truth. At the same time, you cannot violate a dozen other Biblical and moral principles in order to meet your obligations to the church and expect God to bail you out of your trouble because you are giving above and beyond your means to give.

Many televangelists lead their sheep astray with the idea that no matter what circumstances a person finds himself in, he can deal with God by giving to the respective ministry on air. Faith healers are masters at this. Of course, every now and then, one of them gets caught fleecing the flock and goes off to jail. I have found this to be the case over and over in my life.

Many people who come to me for counseling are head over heels in debt, drowning in the perdition of materialism. As Christians, they have gotten themselves deeper into trouble financially by giving away their hard-earned money to someone they see on television who has convinced them that a donation to the ministry will ease them out of their troubles.

Older people are especially vulnerable to this message. Popular television ministries are supported in part by older people who give their Social Security checks to these ministries in order to get God's blessings.

It is true that the widow woman in the gospels who gave her last two "mites" into the offering was commended by Jesus for her sacrifice. But I do not believe he would have noted her deed had she not been financially responsible otherwise.

If I had it to do over again, I would have spent more of my time educating people not to give to people or ministries they can't see, feel, or touch. With the right kind of teaching, Christians who have become dysfunctional financially would get their individual houses in order so that the money they give each Sunday to the Lord would not be stolen from creditors they have not paid.

When you get old, you are going to need money. At some point in your life, you are not going to be able to work. How do you solve this problem? By saving money early in life for the future and by not wasting what you have in the present. It's as simple as that.

"But I don't have enough money to save," you say. When you have worked at getting your priorities turned around, you will have some money to put aside.

## Four Ways to Financial Security

**1. Earn your way bit-by-bit**

**2. Save one dollar at a time**

**3. Keep your financial priorities in order**

**4. Accept full responsibility for all decisions**

If you follow these suggestions, you will have enough money for a secure and prosperous future.

### 1. Earn Your Way

Don't try to accomplish everything in one bite. Work your way to financial security by being patient. If you try to make it big on one deal, you will probably end up frustrated as well as broke. Chip away piece by piece until your goals are accomplished.

One of the things that is wrong with our young people today is they are trying to bite off too big a piece of the pie all at once. They want it all too soon.

It gets frustrating sometimes when I am advising young businessmen to slow down and take some baby steps, and they won't listen. I have discovered that when one of these young men is failing at business, it is usually because he is hunting elephants instead of squirrels.

I have to sit him down and say, "Don't try to make all your money in one deal. If you are patient and bring on many smaller clients, these will pay real dividends when you do stumble onto a bigger client. Put enough hooks in the water, and you will eventually catch a big fish."

This advice goes for everyone whether you are trying to reach your financial goals by buying property, investing in the markets, or working a moonlight job. Dividends are paid by patience.

## 2. Save One Dollar at a Time

"I don't save money because I do not have enough to save," a lady once said to me after one of my lectures.

"How much do you have?" I asked curiously. "Do you have anything left over after you pay all your bills?"

Her reply was, "I have about $100 a month, but that is not enough to save to amount to anything — so I spend it."

"How old are you?" I boldly asked.

"Twenty five," she replied suspiciously.

"Believe me, $100 is indeed plenty to save," I said. "If you save $1200 per year for 40 years, you will have lots of money."

Associated Press business writer Chet Currier put forth this scenario in his March 17, 1996 column:

"If a 40-year-old worker puts $2,000 annually into a tax-free municipal bond fund earning a 6 percent return, at age 60 he or she will have $155,000. If that same $2,000 is contributed annually to an IRA and invested in a stock fund with a 10 percent return, at age 60 the kitty will be worth $325,000. To retire comfortably, most people will need to save at least $2,000 per year in addition to their company and/or self-employed retirement plan contributions."

If you are reading this book during the 2009 recession, when this book was published, you probably think I'm nuts. Keep in mind the markets will return and the profits will be earned.

Too often we wait until it is late in life to start saving for our retirement. We then have to make it up quickly, which causes a great deal of stress and discontent. At that point, it's easy to fall prey to risky deals. Many people try to make quick dollars and end up losing it all.

Find a comfort range for saving money and start somewhere. Discipline yourself to do this every week.

This very night, while I am writing this chapter, a lady called and asked how much I thought she should try and save.

I said, "Ten percent."

"I can't do that," she replied.

"Then start with one percent and work your way up to ten."

That made her feel good. She could start somewhere and feel good about what she was doing.

Financial security cannot be reached without a plan for saving money.

### 3. Keep Your Financial Priorities in Order

The sum total of what you will accomplish financially depends on how you ration the money you have.

Years ago, I was talking to a man in our church and asked him, "Why won't people commit themselves to giving to the church?"

I was very young and just starting out my adult life.

"I don't understand why people would use all the facilities of the church and allow other people to pay for them," I said innocently.

The man's answer has stuck with me all these years. "When it gets right down to it," he replied frankly, "people do exactly what they want to do. Nothing more, nothing less."

Life requires that we do a lot of thinking about how we are going to live. Because of this, we make choices. Successes in life depend upon the sum total of the choices we have made — good and bad. The more bad choices we make, the less successes we will achieve; the more good choices, the better off we can make our lives.

This principle is also true of moral choices. We can choose good ways and bad ways. People in prisons made bad choices.

Magic Johnson was the idol of millions of kids who love the game of basketball. He had everything the world has to offer, but he made a bad choice. He chose to have illicit relationships with women, which got him AIDS and could eventually get him a premature death.

Whether you agree with that lifestyle or you don't is not the issue. The issue is that Magic made some regretful choices that have cost him his health and a lot of sorrow.

Choice is the most powerful weapon in man's arsenal. Animals do not have this privilege. The duck doesn't choose to fly south. The bear can't decide it won't hibernate and instead take the winter off and go to Florida with the cubs (little bears, not the baseball team). Not one creature in the animal kingdom makes moral choices. They live and die by instinct.

Man is the only part of God's creation that is different. We have the opportunity to choose the direction our lives will take, and that is a powerful gift.

Mankind has the power of choice but not the power over the consequences of that choice. When we decide to do something or not do something, we have made the decision. We do not, however, have power over the outcome of that decision. That is left up to the circumstances surrounding the results of the decision.

When we are making financial decisions, the outcome will be either costly or profitable. If we make a decision to buy a new home or a new car, we have to calculate the cost and determine whether we can afford it or not. If we covet something we cannot afford, and plunge deeply into debt to get it, that will affect us for the rest of our lives. Almost every decision we make in life has financial consequences.

My son Scott told me the other day he does not take his wife Debbie to the grocery store if both of them have not eaten. His theory is that they will spend more money on food if their stomachs are empty. That makes sense!

To be financially burden-free, you must line up your priorities. What is the most important issue you are facing in your life? It is probably where you work and how much you are being paid.

All your decisions financially are predicated upon how much you are bringing home from the job you have. Because of this, it is required that a certain amount of your pay check go for life's necessities. If you get your priorities messed up, then you will not have enough money to maintain your lifestyle.

How does that happen? By paying for things that are not priority items with money generally targeted for necessary expenses. This is why people get into trouble and are short of capital.

We need to set boundaries for ourselves. When a football player catches a punt and starts running toward the goal at the opposite end of the football field, he must stay within certain boundaries to not be penalized. He cannot take the ball and run up in the stands to avoid being tackled and then run back onto the football field. He must pay strict attention to the rules and guidelines while he is moving toward the goal line.

Our financial decisions must be approached in the same way. We can't take our money and run with it any way we want. We must have parameters to keep ourselves from being penalized, and if we stay within those limits, we will safely and successfully reach our goals in life.

### 4. Accept Full Accountability for All Decisions

It is easy to blame someone else for all our problems. One of the worst financial messes I have ever seen came recently as I sat and talked with a couple who had four small children. The gentleman had been in business for 18 years working on his own time and billing for the labor.

As his business grew, he began taking on contracts that required bids for labor and materials. He had gotten along fine billing by the hour or job labor, but when the bids included material, he was seeing much more money per contract. He would get paid, and the material bills did not come due until the next month. Cash accumulated quickly, and suddenly he had an abundance of it.

The lure of so much cash caused the couple to increase their spending. As the material bills came due, they were able to stay ahead for awhile. Then, like an unseen tidal wave that starts far out in the ocean, the surge of bills came like a tsunami rolling in and drowned them.

As I looked over their situation, I analyzed what had happened. I was not pulling him out of the way of an approaching breaker: I was digging in the sand, trying to find him buried under it.

This couple had not filed an income tax return for three years because they were afraid the IRS would put them in jail because they couldn't pay their income tax. The IRS doesn't do this because it is not lawful to jail anyone for debt in this country, including what you owe the government as income tax — unless the government can prove you are committing fraud.

The crime concerning personal or proprietary income is the failure to file income tax, not the failure to pay it. If you file and do not pay your taxes with the filing forms, the IRS becomes a creditor and must collect the debt just like anyone else. As you probably remember reading earlier in this book, the IRS has more power than any other creditor in the United States, so collecting the debt is not a problem.

The man in question had gotten so far behind in keeping his records and had so many judgments against him for not paying his suppliers that there was nothing he could do. The situation was hopeless.

How did he get in such a mess? During the initial stages of our conversation, this man tried to evade the reasons for his troubles then he finally understood that his troubles stemmed from the fact that he had no accountability to himself for record keeping, budgeting, or spending. It was easy to blame the industry and his circumstances, but in the end he realized he was out of focus, out of balance, and must "cash in the chips" and take his losses.

Unfortunately, when he filed bankruptcy, his suppliers took their losses as well.

## One Last Bit of Advice

How do you view life? If you've lived long enough, you have probably realized that life is not what we think it is. We are told things are one way only to find out they are quite another.

What contributes to this disillusionment of life? Television, radio, and movies are big factors. Before television, we all read more. Because of the visual transformation of seeing things in pictures, our opinions are formulated by a writer's perception — which may or may not be reality.

For many years, we have been brainwashed into a world of

unreality. The financial pressures most of us have experienced are formulated by unrealistic dreams put into our minds by endless commercials preaching the dogma that we must have anything we want at any price we are willing to pay.

The great economist, Adam Smith — who has framed much of my biased sentiments — writes: "Image, reality, and identity bring anxiety about money, and if that won't scare you off, nothing will."

Money is very serious business. Most of us who have never had much of it know the truth in this statement.

It is part of our Christian ethnic to treat money at times as something taboo and at other times to indulge ourselves as if we were bathing in liquid silver and gold. Nothing else in life gets quite that much attention from us.

It is funny how we treat money. In one moment, it is used to make more money. In the next, it is thrown away brazenly on gaming tables at casinos, and the earnings hidden away in secret bank accounts. Money is used to purchase outlandish homes, flashy cars, fashionable clothes, and gaudy jewelry, yet when asked how much money one has, it becomes so esoteric that the possessor doesn't dare talk about it.

We romance money, or we want nothing to do with it. We count it, keep up with it, get frustrated with it, or we park it in the hands of a money manager and forget it. Regardless of how we treat our money, there is a large portion of literature out there that wants to tell us how to deal with it. This book is no different.

I didn't write this book to make money, and I won't belabor the point. Authors are sometimes like poets. They starve to death laboring over a manuscript in some attic, and then 400 years after they are dead, someone discovers its value.

All of our ambitions, dreams, and hopes are predicated by the use of money. Sometimes circumstances and acts of God keep our programs from working as we have planned. Therefore there is no book, not even this one, that can guarantee success.

Whether you have a portfolio of stocks and bonds, have money in the bank or no money at all, my prayer is that everyone who reads this book will learn something — and in some way bring about a happy ending to everyone who absorbs it.

One last bit of advice: Diversify your life just like you should your money. Otherwise, you may become like the man who, out of thousands of stocks in which to invest, picked the very one that permitted him to lose every penny.

# APPENDIX

# WORKS CITED

## Chapter 1

Figgie, Harry E., and Gerald J. Swanson. *Bankruptcy 1995: The Coming Collapse of America and How to Stop It.* Boston: Little, Brown Publishers, 1993.

Carson, Clarence B. *Basic Economics.* Wadley, AL: Textbook Committee, 1988.

Lynch, Peter, John Rothchild. *Beating the Street.* 1994.

Smith, James B. *Business Law in California,* 11th Edition. General Education Publications, 1984.

Burkett, Larry. *The Coming Economic Earthquake.* Chicago: Moody Press, 1992.

Davis, Michele Weiner. *"Divorce Busting: A Revolutionary and Rapid Program for Staying Together."* Fireside Publication.

Smith, Sherman S. *"The End of the Cold War and Its Effect on the Economy in the 1990s."* Video, Liberty Broadcasting Network.

Benna, R. Theodore, and William Proctor, Theodore R. Benna. *Escaping the Coming Retirement Crisis: How to Secure Your Financial Future.* 1995.

McArthur, John. *"God's Plan for Giving."* Word of Grace Publishers.

Jr. Dent, Harry S. *Great Boom Ahead*. New York: Hyperion, 1993.

Burkett, Larry. *How to Prosper in the Underground Economy: A Completely Legal Guide to the Hidden, Multibillion-Dollar Cash Economy*. William Morrow & Company, 1982.

## Chapter 2

Morley, Patrick M. *The Man in the Mirror*. Nashville: Thomas Nelson Publisher, 1992.

Nance, Wayne, and Dr. Ed Charlesworth. *Mind Over Money*. Nashville: Thomas Nelson Publisher, 1993.

Smith, Adam. *The Money Game*. Random House, 1965.

Hansen, George. *"To Harass Our People: The IRS and Government Abuse of Power."* Positive Publications, 1984.

Jr. Dayton, Howard L. *Your Money: Frustration or Freedom*. Tyndale House Publishers. 1994.

References for quoted mater alma.

## Chapter 3

Jr. Dayton, Howard L. *Your Money: Frustration or Freedom*. Tyndale House Publishers. 1994.

McArthur, John. *"God's Plan for Giving."* Word of Grace Publishers: 30.

Nance, Wayne, and Dr. Ed Charlesworth. *Mind Over Money*. Nashville: Thomas Nelson Publisher, 1993.

Smith, Adam. *The Money Game*. Random House, 1965: 301–302.

## Chapter 4

Figgie, Harry E., and Gerald J. Swanson. *Bankruptcy 1995: The Coming Collapse of America and How to Stop It*. Boston: Little, Brown Publishers, 1993.

## Chapter 5

Davis, Michele Weiner. "Divorce Busting a Revolutionary and Rapid Program for Staying Together." Fireside Publications, quoted in Bottom Line March 15, 1996.

## Chapter 7

Benna, R. Theodore, and William Proctor, Theodore R. Benna. *Escaping the Coming Retirement Crisis: How to Secure Your Financial Future.* 1995: pg. 9.

## Chapter 8

Hansen, George. *"To Harass Our People: The IRS and Government Abuse of Power."* Positive Publications, 1984.

Jensen and Wiggins. *CPA Tax Letter.* Jan. Feb. March, 1996: 3.

## Chapter 9

Peter Lynch and John Rothschild. *Worth Magazine* September, 1995, pg. 80.

Judy Meehan quoted by Thomas Olson, *"Bears Ready to Prowl?"* Pittsburgh Tribune Review March 9, 1996.

Tony Spare quoted in *"Market's Jumpiness is Really Not All That New."*

Patricia Lamiell, *Pittsburgh Tribune Review* March 3 1996.

Lynch, Peter, John Rothchild. *Beating the Street.* 1994.

Jr. Salomon, R.S. *Forbes* Dec. 4 1995: 288.

Steven H. Hanke, *"Turmoil in Europe,"* Forbes Nov. 20 1995: 64.

Jr. Dent, Harry S. *Great Boom Ahead.* New York: Hyperion, 1993: 163.

Forbes, Malcolm. *Forbes* Dec. 16, 1985.

Tanzer, Andrew. *"China's Ravenous Appetite,"* Forbes Dec. 18 1995: 148.

Liu Yonghoa quoted *"Capitalist Pigs."* Forbes January 1 1996: 54.

Richard Nixon quoted by Harry S. Dent. *The Great Boom Ahead.* New York: Hyperion, 1993: 77.

Burkett, Larry. *The Coming Economic Earthquake.* Chicago: Moody Press, 1992: 153, 59.

Figgie, Harry E. *Bankruptcy* 1995. Boston: Little, Brown, & Co, 1992: 74, 75.

Smith, Sherman S. *"The End of the Cold War and Its Effect on the Economy in the 1990s."* Video, Liberty Broadcasting Network.

## Chapter 10

Burkett, Larry. *How to Prosper in the Underground Economy: A Completely Legal Guide to the Hidden, Multibillion-Dollar Cash Economy.* William Morrow & Company, 1982: 208, 207, 208, 209.

Carson, Clarence B. *Basic Economics.* ATC Publishers, 1988: 312.

## Chapter 11

Reprint from Fortune Magazine, July 6 1987. *"The Money Society."* Source: Morley, Patrick M. The Man in the Mirror. Thomas Nelson Publisher, 1992: 132.